MUSLIM CONTRIBUTIONS
TO WORLD CIVILIZATION

THE INTERNATIONAL INSTITUTE OF ISLAMIC THOUGHT
P.O. BOX 126, RICHMOND, SURREY TW9 2UD, UK

HEAD OFFICE
P.O. BOX 669, HERNDON, VA 22070, USA

ISBN 1–56564–410–7 paperback
ISBN 1–56564–411–5 hardback

Typeset by Sohail Nakhooda
Cover design by Saddiq Ali
Printed in the United Kingdom by Biddles Limited, King's Lynn

CONTENTS

FOREWORD

The International Institute of Islamic Thought (IIIT) in cooperation with the Association of Muslim Social Scientists (AMSS) has great pleasure in presenting this small volume highlighting Islam's intellectual legacy to world civilization.

Islam's brilliant contributions to science, art, and culture, are a timeless and precious heritage, which should be historically preserved for future generations. The great achievements of Muslim scholars are rarely if at all acknowledged in formal education, and today their identity, origins and impact remain largely obscure. This collection of papers aims to give readers a brief introduction to the intellectual history of Muslims and the contributions that eminent Muslim scholars have made in certain specific fields of knowledge including basic and applied physical and biological sciences, medicine, legal and political theories and practices, economic and financial concepts, models, and institutions, etc. It does not include Muslim contributions to several other fields like language and literature, fine arts, and architecture, which call for a separate volume on the subject.

The preservation of civilization necessitates a better understanding, sharing, and recognition of our common human heritage. Given today's widespread negative stereotyping and falsely generated misunderstanding of Islam and Muslims, the publication of these papers on "Muslim Contributions to World Civilization" is vital to help repair the wrong that is being perpetrated and restore the historical truth, which is being distorted.

The IIIT, established in 1981, has served as a major center to facilitate sincere and serious scholarly efforts based on Islamic vision, values and principles. Its programs of research, seminars and conferences during the last twenty four years have resulted in the publication of more than two hundred and fifty titles in English and Arabic, many of which have been translated into several other languages.

The AMSS (USA) was founded in 1972 to provide a forum through which Islamic positions on various academic disciplines can be promoted. The AMSS has based its activities on the belief that the development of Islamic thought is vital for the prosperity of the Muslim world and for the continuity of the Islamic intellectual heritage. Since its development in the USA a number of other similar associations have been established in the UK, France, Germany, and India.

We would like to express our thanks to Dr. Dilnawaz A. Siddiqui who throughout the various stages of the book's production cooperated closely with us. We would also like to thank the editorial and production team at the London Office and those who were directly or indirectly involved in the completion of this book: Hagga Abugideiri, Linda Barto, Sylvia Hunt, Shiraz Khan, Maryam Mahmood, Sohail Nakhooda and, Riyad al-Yemany. May God reward them, the authors, and the editors for all their efforts.

Rabiᶜ II 1426   ANAS AL-SHAIKH-ALI
June 2005   *Academic Advisor*
                                              IIIT London Office, UK

PREFACE

T HE PRIMARY GOAL of this volume is to give readers a brief introduction to the intellectual history of Muslims and their contributions to civilization. Civilization itself developed long before the nineteenth century and, since time immemorial, many peoples have woven the fabric, each making its own unique contribution. This book highlights the contributions that Muslim scholars made in the various fields of human endeavor, including science, technology, philosophy, and the political and social sciences from 700 to 1500 AC. These breakthroughs went on to constitute a firm foundation for progress in the Near East, North Africa, and Spain, eventually leading to the European Renaissance during the middle of the second millennium and beyond. The preservation of civilization necessitates a better understanding, sharing, and recognition of our common human heritage.

Given today's widespread negative stereotyping and media-generated misunderstanding of Islam and Muslims, the publication of the topic "Muslim Contributions to World Civilization" is vital to repair the wrong that is being done and restore the historical truth, which is being distorted. Mainstream Western history concerning the advancement of knowledge acknowledges the work done by Greek and Roman scholars until around 300 AC and then conveniently jumps to 1500 AC, the age of the European Renaissance, with very little mention of the stunning and far-reaching social, political, and scientific developments which took place from the eighth to the sixteenth century AC. Morowitz, a historian, describes this phenomenon as "History's Black Hole." "The impression given is that the Renaissance arose phoenix-like from the ashes – smoldering for a millennium – of the classical age of Greece and Rome."[1] This is a myth that gives an extremely distorted view of history. An adequate knowledge of the contributions of Islam and Muslims to civilization helps to counteract the widely propagated contemporary false image of Muslims in the West as being violent, barbaric and anti-civilizational. To understand the high and breathtakingly enlightened culture of the Muslim "Golden Age" is to understand the positive part that Muslims played, and indeed, continue to play in the development of advanced human society.

During the height of the Islamic period, from 700 to 1500 AC, the world witnessed a major development in the arts and sciences. As a result of the extent of the rapidly expanding Islamic empire, Muslim scholars inherited the knowledge of nearly all of the other hitherto major civilizations: ancient Egyptian, Babylonian, Greek, Persian, and Indian. Caliphs and scholars made massive efforts to translate these sources into Arabic. Many important scientific and philosophical treatises were thus preserved from extinction. Not only did the Muslim scholars learn and preserve the knowledge of antiquity, but they also made their own critical observations and original research, thus adding a vast treasure of new scientific knowledge in the fields of philosophy, astronomy, history, mathematics, chemistry, and the medical sciences, to name but a few.

As Muslim intellectuals, it is our responsibility to research and publish this original work and to disseminate as widely as possible the great historical legacy of these giants of their time so that the world does not forget them, but recognizes and honors their contributions to science, knowledge, and civilization. Several nationally known scholars and authorities on the subject have contributed to this project by analyzing various aspects of Muslim scholars' contributions to human civilization. The project covers a wide range of subjects, including Muslim contributions to the political system, social sciences, humanities, jurisprudence, medical sciences, and especially the impact of Islam on the West.

AbdulHamid AbuSulayman eloquently stresses that Islam and Christianity, two of the greatest religions of the Abrahamic legacy, have made significant contributions to human civilization. At this juncture when our world is akin to a global village, an understanding of the common origins of all faith communities, especially of the two largest ones, is absolutely necessary to restore humankind to its senses. One important method of achieving this aim is to tackle and solve the problems created by a distorted and volatile history. A measure of desperately needed cross-cultural harmony can be accomplished by a better understanding of the contributions that numerous scholars and followers of these great religions have made throughout history. Recognition of their sincere dedication to pristine spiritual, moral, and ethical values and an emulation of their legacy can certainly help to achieve the worthy goal of global peace and justice.

Syed Ahsani's article outlines the Islamic political system with a case study of al-Māwardī's Paradigm. Following Western domination of the Muslim countries, Islamic thinkers have reacted on three different levels to comparative political systems. First, the apologists have advocated the adoption of the Western model of democracy. Second, the Traditionalists, on the other hand, have argued that this policy would lead to secularization, thus compromising Islamic values. Lastly, the moderates have stressed the middle-of-the-road position benefiting from Western learning as the lost heritage of Islam, yet at the same time observing the fundamentals of Islamic Shariᶜah.

These divisions are not new: they existed in the Abbasid period when the Muᶜtazilites rationalists gave primacy to reason. The rise of Philosophy under Caliph al-Maᶜmūn inspired fear among religious scholars that Revelation might be threatened by Reason, which gave rise to two kinds of reaction: *Ahl al-Ḥadīth* or the Traditionalists, who totally rejected reason, and the Ashaᶜrites, who put limits on it to save Revelation from being rejected. Māwardī, a Muslim intellectual, criticized the established practice that Shariᶜah (Islamic Law) by itself was a sufficient yardstick for justice. His greatest contribution was the introduction of the concept of political justice into the Shariᶜah .

Dilnawaz A. Siddiqui in his chapter titled, "Middle Eastern Origins of Modern Sciences," traces the roots of an explosion of knowledge which took place in the entire Muslim world from the late Umayyad era through the Abbasid era and into the fifteenth century. He attributes this unprecedented phenomenon to the Divine injunctions contained in the Qur'an that Muslim men and Muslim women should study the books, that is, the Qur'an, and the universe, each in light of the other. In other words, that it was one's Islamic duty to enhance continually one's understanding of all of God's creation. The acute consciousness of their duty enabled Muslims to strike a balance between reason and Revelation. The Islamic principle of monogenesis inspired them not only to benefit from the collective wisdom of all times and climes but also to create a societal order characterized by open access to all levels of knowledge for all of humanity, regardless of gender, race, ethnicity, religion, or national origin. This

climate of social equality engendered and disseminated a spirit of universal brotherhood, leading to creative and innovative ways of learning,
including the scientific method of observation, and thus to the evolution of
various disciplines of knowledge. His chapter deals with Muslim contributions to the humanities, mathematics, basic and applied natural and
social sciences, and also gives in tabular form the names, dates, and significant works of the major Muslim scholars of the eight centuries covered.

In Chapter 6, M. Basheer Ahmed's "Contributions of Muslim Physicians and Other Scholars from 700 to 1600 AC," highlights the fact that
Muslim scholars were at the cutting edge of scientific development during
that period. As leaders of this knowledge, they thus exercised a profound
influence over the history of humankind. He points out that their works
were of the highest quality, demonstrating the hallmarks of good science:
experiment, observation, rationality, objectivity and professionalism.
Their works demonstrated superbly the absence of a conflict between
faith and science, a division that continued to dog the Christian world
until secularization freed the thinking of its scientists from Church
dogma. The scientific legacy of the Muslims laid the foundations for the
progress of science and technology in Europe in the second millennium.
Europe had hitherto been languishing in what is now termed the "Dark
Ages," and it is by no means an exaggeration to state that it was Europe's
encounter with Muslims and Muslim civilization that became the engine
of the European Renaissance. The works of Muslim scholars were widely
used as textbooks in many European universities until 1600 AC. The
Arabic texts were translated into Latin and other European languages.
The universities of Iraq, Syria, Egypt, Spain, Iran, Córdoba, Cairo, etc.
became the major teaching centers of the world, where students flocked
from all over Europe to study. Famous physicians, like al-Rāzī (Rhazes)
and Ibn Sīna (Avicenna) had their encyclopedic works on medicine taught
in European universities until the sixteenth century. As Briffault, a
historian, writes: "what we call science arose as a result of new methods
of experiments, observation and measurements which were introduced
into Europe by Muslims. Modern science is based on the most monumental contribution of the Islamic civilization."[2] Ahmed briefly describes
the work of several physicians in that era.

Louay M. Safi, an intellectual who has had the opportunity to experience both Muslim and non-Muslim cultures, points out in Chapter 2,

"Overcoming the Religious-Secular Divide: Islam's Contribution to Civilization," that the future of human civilization is directly linked to our ability to learn from the historical experience of both Islamic and Western civilization. He writes,

> Although Islamic and Western civilizations appear to be far removed from each other at the level of structure and organization, both seem to share a common commitment to the universal values of social justice, equality, common good, social welfare, political participation, religious freedom, and a host of other common principles and values. Western civilization has perfected the structural elements of social life so as to allow a better integration of the above universal values into social organization. Western successes were, however, achieved by overcoming two major historical forces that are peculiar to the West: feudalism and organized religion. This fact has contributed to the erosion of the very moral basis in which Western Renaissance is rooted – Enlightened religiosity... a political order rooted in Islamic norms shares with the modern secularist orders its desire to liberate the body politic from narrow religious and cultural interpretations. Unlike the secularist order, the Islamic political order, however, encourages the fostering of moral values in accordance with the overall scheme of moral autonomy.

In Chapter 4, "Intellectual History of Euro-American Jurisprudence: and the Islamic Alternative," Peter M. Wright compares and contrasts the contemporary legal systems prevailing in Europe, the Americas, and in the former European colonies with the principles of Islamic Shariᶜah. He asserts that the Western legal systems have "evolved in specific historical contexts and cultural milieus. Nevertheless, they share certain common presumptions that are rarely articulated or exposed to critical scrutiny." Wright's chapter might be a beginning in the process of articulating in a cogent manner common presumptions behind current European legal structures. It is an "attempt to constructively engage them through a comparative study of a rival legal system such as may be found in accepted principles of Islamic Shariᶜah."

In Chapter 7, Mohammed Sharif discusses "The Feasibility of an Islamic Economic System in a Modern Economy". He points out that the modern economic system has become complex and is becoming more so, to the extent that its problems are almost intractable. He states that this is so only because it denies one very important aspect of human life, namely, the soul (spirit) and that it seeks to direct the whole system toward a fierce competition to gain as many material possessions and as much power as possible. The secular modern society creates many problems and is absolutely ill-equipped to deal with them. The only thing it does is to enact more and more laws with stringent punishment for violation, but to no avail; the allure of material possession and power is much too great to keep the aspirants to material success from violating the laws. In contrast, the Islamic system is simple and straightforward enough for everyone to understand. Moreover, its spiritual guidance is persuasive enough to make humanity abide by its Divine injunctions, which are universally beneficial. It gears society towards creating and maintaining the environment for both the material and spiritual upliftment of all members of society. If the Islamic system is applied, it can successfully eliminate the problems of the complex modern economy in straightforward and simple ways and can lead to economic development, rather than growth.

Abdel-Hameed M. Bashir continues the subject of an Islamic economic system in his, "Islamic Financial Institutions in the USA: Viability and Prospects." Islam is the first religion to introduce an interest-free lending system. The Islamic financial system, based on participation and risk-sharing, offers a viable remedy for the world debt crisis. Under Islamic modes of financing, the lender is expected to share part of the risk in investing. Accordingly, Islamic financing encourages active participation and asserts that money borrowed is not entitled to a reward. Thus the system of shared risk is expected to reduce the possibility of financial crises and to be more fair and equitable. Hence, Muslims are encouraged to abide by the tenets of Islam and not to deal with interest because of the great torment that awaits those who practice usury. Therefore, it is imperative for Muslims in the West in general, and the United States in particular, to establish financial institutions that provide them with interest-free choices.

Multiple factors were responsible for the eventual decline in scientific progress in the Muslim world. They included the foreign invasion of Baghdad by the Mongols, the invasion of Syria and Palestine by the Crusaders, and the loss of Muslim Spain, resulting in the demise of the world's renowned teaching and research centers. Subsequently, two parallel systems of education were developed, namely, the Shariʿah, the science of Islamic jurisprudence, and al-ʿUlūm al-ʿAqliyyah, natural science and technology. The new schools which came into being as a result, *madāris* (sing. *madrasah*), discouraged the teaching of science and technology and focused only on theology, and the spiritual and ritual aspects of Islam. These were the major reasons for the disincentive amongst the new Muslim generation to acquire new knowledge and conduct scientific research. Religious fanaticism, narrow-mindedness, and a lack of tolerance finally resulted in the marked lack of progress in this area.

Science does not belong to a particular ethnic or religious group. It is an evolutionary process that will continue to progress fuelled by contributions from different races and groups. We hope that this book will become a source of inspiration for all Muslims, especially the young, to make their own scholarly stamp on history and the development of human civilization.

M. BASHEER AHMED

PROLOGUE

THE HISTORY of the advancement of knowledge in Europe and the United States acknowledges the work done by Greek and Roman scholars until around 300 AC and then picks up the trail again in 1500 AC – the beginning of the Renaissance. There is very little mention of the history of social, political or scientific development during the period 300–1500 AC. Morowitz describes this phenomenon as "History's Black Hole," that the Renaissance somehow arose like a "phoenix" from the "ashes," which had been smouldering for a millennium since "the classical age of Greece and Rome."[1]

In reality, during the height of the Islamic period from 700 to 1500 AC, the world witnessed a major development in the arts and sciences. Muslim scholars learned from the scholarly works of the Greeks and Romans, and saved them from extinction by translating them into Arabic. They also critiqued and improved them, and finally passed them on to posterity, thus facilitating the ushering in of the European Renaissance. Europe was in a dire state, for scientific, medical, academic, and scholarly work had virtually stopped for one thousand years. One of the main reasons for this stagnation was the anti-intellectualism of Church dogma. Most of the work done by Greek and some Roman scholars had remained dormant during this interregnum. The burning of the great library of Alexandria in 390 AC by fundamentalist Christians resulted in the loss of a vast amount of classical heritage.

Muslim scholars not only gave new life to these works but also made their own observations and original research, adding to this legacy a vast treasure of new scientific knowledge in the fields of philosophy, astronomy, history, mathematics, chemistry, and the medical sciences. The contributions of Muslim scientists show the highest quality of scientific development in the Muslim world. Their original research work and brilliant contributions proved that philosophy, sciences, and theology could be harmonized as a unified whole and that Islam did not subscribe to any contradiction between true faith and tried and tested science.

To give a brief overview: Arab Muslims transmitted the zero from India to the world; Leonardo Da Vinci studied the Arabic numeral system and introduced it to Europe; algorithm (algorism) was invented by al-Khawārizmī in the ninth century, and Abū al-Wafā developed trigonometry. Ibn al-Haytham developed optics, proving that rays pass from objects into the eye, and wrote about optic illusions, binocular vision, mirages, rainbows, and halos. Jābbir ibn Ḥayyān prepared sulphuric acid and classified chemicals in the eighth century. Paper-manufacturing technology was brought by Muslims in the ninth century and spread to the Middle East and Europe, leading to an expansion in the publication of books. The Muslim scholar Ibn Khaldūn is credited with founding the discipline of sociology. Al-Idrīsī, who lived in Sicily, compiled a book on medieval history and the geography of Europe, producing 70 maps of the world. Al-Bayrūnī and Ibn Baṭūṭah were famous travelers and historians, whose scholarly works are still regarded as pioneering contributions to history and geography.

The best Islamic hospitals were several centuries in advance of European hospitals. In teaching methods, they exerted a strong influence, and the Arab practice of taking students on ward rounds in the hospitals attached to the medical schools has been rediscovered many times from medical schools in Salerano to Sir William Osler at the end of the nineteenth century in Canadian, British, and US schools. The Arab teaching methods have remained part of the standard system of medical studies in Western medical schools.

In medicine, Ibn al-Nafīs al-Qarshī of Damascus charted and explained the circulation of blood, three centuries before William Harvey discovered the same; al-Rāzī differentiated between measles and smallpox; and al-Ṭabarī realized that tuberculosis was an infection. In Spain, al-Zahrāwī invented surgical instruments, removed cataracts, and perfected many surgical procedures. Ibn Zuhr started suturing wounds with silk thread.

It was in pharmacology that Muslim physicians made the most lasting contribution. They not only discovered many herbal drugs but also perfected many of the techniques of chemical extraction that we know today, including filtration, distillation, and crystallization. In seventeenth century England, the great work of systematizing drugs, *The Pharmacopoeia of the London College of Physicians* (1618), was illustrated with portraits of a few great scholars and these included Hypocrites, Galen, Avicenna (Ibn Sīna), and Mesuë (Ibn Zakariyyah bin Masawayh).

Muslim physicians undertook and accomplished the monumental task of producing the first classical medical textbooks in a format which would be recognizable to medical students even today. These textbooks were based as much on original Greek works as on the new scientific data gathered by Muslim physicians. The most famous academicians and scholars who helped in producing such works were al-Rāzī (Rhazes, 932), al-Zahrāwī (1013) and Ibn Sīna (1092).

Muslim scientists and scholars introduced scientific knowledge to Europe at a time when Europe was enveloped in what is known as the "Dark Ages." Muslim scholars were the leading lights of scientific development between 700 and 1500 AC, and exercised a profound influence upon the history of humankind. Their scientific legacy laid the foundations for the progress of science and technology in Europe in the second millennium. Indeed, these scholars played a vital role in the evolution of human civilization and served as the true harbingers of Europe's Renaissance. Their works were used as textbooks in many European universities until 1600 AC. The works of Muslim scholars in Arabic were translated into Latin and other European languages and students flocked from all over Europe to study at the universities of Baghdad, Spain, Syria, Cairo, and Iran, which became the major teaching centers of the world. The writings of famous physicians, like al-Rāzī and Ibn Sīna's encyclopedic work on medicine, were taught in European universities until the sixteenth century. Morowitz further states that history as taught in the United States is presented as having a cultural black hole in the Middle Ages. This is a myth that gives a very distorted picture and a very historically inaccurate view.

George Sarton (1947),[2] dealing with Muslim scholars, wrote that during the period 750 to 1150 AC the contributions of Muslim scholars were unmatched in their brilliance and included such intellectual giants as al-Rāzī, al-Fārābī, Ibn al-Haytham, al-Khawārizmī, Ibn Sīna, al-Bayrūnī and Ibn Khaldūn. Briffault writes:

> What we call science arose as a result of new methods of experiments, observation and measurement which were introduced into Europe by Arabs. Modern science is the most momentous contribution of the Islamic civiliza-

tion, which was made accessible to all regardless of gender, race, caste, creed, or national origin.[3]

The first regional conference of the Association of Muslim Social Scientists was held in Dallas, Texas in June 2001, on the theme "Muslim Contributions to Human Civilization." The objective of the conference was to introduce to both Muslim and non-Muslim audiences the great contributions that Muslim scientists and scholars have made to humankind. Human civilization was not developed in the nineteenth century or in 400 BC, nor is it the exclusive preserve of a particular group of people. Many people have woven the fabric of human civilization since time immemorial. It is like constructing a building to which every nation and ethnic group have contributed their share of materials and expertise. This particular conference highlighted the scholarly and scientific knowledge of Muslims in the Middle Ages, which led to the eventual Renaissance of Europe and the rise of the West to its present heights. Its preservation lies in a better understanding, sharing, and recognition of our common heritage.

Several nationally known speakers and authorities on this subject participated in the conference. Presented in this book is a selection of papers presented at the conference, covering a variety of subjects such as the Islamic contributions to political science, economics, physical and biological sciences, humanities, jurisprudence, medical science, and the impact of Islam on Western thought in general. During the conference, other subjects were also covered. We hope to publish another set of proceedings covering these subjects at a later date.

What the West has Learned from Islamic Civilization

ABDULHAMID ABUSULAYMAN

G IVEN THE CONTEMPORARY social and political climate in the world, it is more significant now than ever before to discuss the contributions of Muslims to civilization, with a view to building bridges of appreciation and understanding among peoples of various cultures and ideologies. A computer search for the need for cross-cultural understanding yields 306,000 web pages.[1]

Having spread all over the world as faith communities, the inheritors of the Abrahamic tradition of monotheism have had the greatest influence on human history.[2] At this juncture of history, when the whole world is like a village, it is of immense importance to work together toward mutual understanding of the common grounds, common goals, and common dedication to the spiritual as well as the moral aspects of life to restore humankind to its senses. The aim is to bring about lasting peace with justice, by resolving problems created by the distortion of history. If there is any way to make real peace in this world, people of the Abrahamic faith trio have a special role to play.[3]

While Christianity and Islam have been behind most of human accomplishments, it is also owing to the distortion of these two faiths that we have faced and are still facing the stupendous problems of global proportions. Christianity with its message of peace and tolerance was distorted so much so that it justified ruthless imperialism and its injustices throughout its colonies in Asia, Africa, and Latin America. Indeed, it was a distortion of that great religion and its spirit. It also gave birth to nationalism, where human beings emphasized only differences that conveniently served the opportunists as a basis for hatred and wars. Its propaganda also contributed to the distortion of Islam and Muslims. Islam came to elevate the human civilization out of the Dark Ages to new heights, and created a new civilization by advanced empirical and experimental sciences as well as by enhancing an awareness of the need for human unity based on the concept of monogenesis.[4]

The lasting spiritual light of Islam immensely impressed people of other faiths so as to change not only their religious beliefs but also their customs and even their languages. It was unprecedented in human history. Northern Arabia, North Africa, and East Africa were not Arabic speaking, which they later became. It was the imprint of these pioneers at a time of darkness, which built the strong foundations of the new civilization, leading to Europe's Protestant revolution (the Reformation), the Renaissance, and the Enlightenment. Deliberate distortions of history have covered up contributions of Islam and Muslims to human civilization.[5] Regrettably, Muslims themselves have little or no idea about their own spiritual light, which has now lost its luster. Consequently, the Muslim people are making little or no significant contribution to the field of modern science today.

To bring genuine peace to this global village, we need to revive the pristine purity and spirit of monotheistic equality and justice for all. We have to ensure that these spiritual values are back in power to bring human beings to their senses. Although the United Nations declared that war was illegal, there were more wars in the world between 1950 and 2000 than ever before. So it is not mere words but also the spirit that brings people together to appreciate one another. The whole idea of Islam, and before that of Christianity, is to bring human beings to this universal spiritual message, to make them identify with one another as creations of the One and Only God (SWT),[6] to serve the good cause in this world, and to achieve eternal happiness in the Hereafter.[7]

In reviving the real values of Christianity, Islam made it clear that human beings are created from a single source (soul). The differences among peoples and the creation of peoples and tribes should not be allowed to lead to conflicts or to seek superiority. Humankind should interact (the Qur'anic word *yata'arraf*) because, if we are all the same or identical, there is no meaning to or method of interaction. When we differ in a positive sense, however, we will interact to contribute to social, economic, and political justice. It is a law of nature for the positive–negative and the male–female to interact to mutual benefit.

Islam does not deny that there are different colors or different languages, yet this is not a cause for determining superiority or inferiority of individual and groups. It is to bring to humankind the wonders of God in creation. So it is a positive phenomenon. According to both Islam and Christianity, justice and personal responsibility are central.[8] We must always do justice to everybody, even to our enemies. What Islam brought forth was religious freedom. Whenever there was a war for the sake of Islam, it was only to bring people their freedom. Whoever agrees to that, shares the goal of peace. Whoever denies human beings the freedom of their own convictions and religion should not be allowed to do so.

In this global village, we need to have the philosophy of peace and freedom to identify and appreciate one another in practice. Real freedom means to be able to do the right thing, and not to do the wrong thing. Freedom without ethics, without values, without a worthy cause, is a curse upon humankind, it is the destruction of civilization. That is where the role of all genuine faith communities comes in: to serve the Divine cause to facilitate life and lend real meaning to it with love, conviction and mutual acceptance.

The Association of Muslim Social Scientists (AMSS) represents the cream of the Muslim communities in the United States. It is the first time, I believe, that there has been an immigration of Muslim intellectuals to this free, influential, and open society. It is the duty of the Muslims in this country, with their intellectual and financial resources, to reform their culture by removing from it all the wrong things which have developed within the Muslim communities. They need to bring back the real values of Islam, and to bring back this kind of moral sense of justice and responsibility.[9] To contribute to this country of theirs and to its people, they ought to unite to serve the good cause of balancing the spiritual and material benefits to humankind.

It is a mission for this Muslim community to seize this opportunity of freedom and resourcefulness to cut the shackles of oppression by dictatorships, to rethink their religion and their culture, and to restore the true light and spirit of the common cause of justice. They also need to work together with their fellow human beings for the benefit of the United States and the world. This country can serve as a vital force for the peace and the prosperity of the whole of humankind, or, with the misuse of its resources, it can become a source of destruction. The power is great, yet it urgently needs strong self-control and proper spiritual guidance. It is up to these faith communities and their cooperation that they can fulfill the mission of peace with justice. It is their duty and an opportunity which they cannot afford to lose. They need to work together for the benefit of humankind, *inshā'Allah*.

Overcoming the Religious-Secular Divide: Islam's Contribution to Civilization

LOUAY M. SAFI

L ANGUAGE is a powerful dimension of social existence and inter-action. It facilitates communication among individuals, and helps create agreement and consensus. It is, as such, an essential tool for advancing both knowledge and society. Nevertheless, language can be also a source of antagonism, misunderstanding, and confusion, and there-fore has the power to undermine social harmony and to close the human mind. The impact of language on thinking and behavior is particularly noticeable when communication and exchange take place across cultures. Under such circumstances, the question of commensurability becomes rel-evant. The question can be posed as thus: Can peoples with different his-torical experiences have a meaningful exchange of ideas, given the fact that understanding the meaning of a term presupposes an experience of a sort of the object to which the term refers? The relationship between knowledge and experience gives rise to a series of questions with regard to understanding the grand concepts of "religion," "secularism," and "liber-alism," and the way each relates to the others. Such terms are not easily and fully interchangeable across cultures and civilizations, and misunder-standing results from extrapolating one's experience across cultures. Thus, superimposing the experience of a historically determined being on another – be it an individual or a community – is bound to stifle or even destroy the latter's chance to develop and mature.

While realizing the above difficulty, I do believe that scholars in general and Muslim scholars in particular are duty-bound to explore meaning across cultures and civilizations, and to stimulate the exchange of ideas and experiences. As a Muslim intellectual who has had the opportunity to experience both Muslim and Western cultures, I do think that the two cultures stand to benefit greatly by learning from each other. I do also think that the future of human civilization is directly linked to our ability to learn from the historical experiences of Islamic and Western civilizations, and our willingness to build on the accomplishments of both.

Although Islamic and Western civilizations appear to be far removed from each other at the level of structure and organization, both seem to share a common commitment to the universal values of social justice, equality, common good, social welfare, political participation, religious freedom, and a host of other common principles and values. Western civilization has perfected the structural elements of social life so as to allow a better integration of the above universal values into social organization. Western successes were, however, achieved by overcoming two major historical forces that are peculiar to the West: feudalism and organized religion. This fact has contributed to the erosion of the very moral basis in which Western Renaissance is rooted – Enlightened religiosity.

Islam, on the other hand, is a tremendous spiritual force in search of modern forms. Historically, Islam is credited with building an outstanding world civilization in which science and religion, and the secular and religious, worked in harmony to advance human life. Can Islam play a similar role in restoring the moral core to modern life and arresting the increasingly immoral and irrational tendencies of the post-modern world? Many Muslim intellectuals would answer this question in the affirmative. The challenge of course is to reinstitute Islamic values and ethos into modern forms. However, for that to happen, Muslim scholars must reconceptualize the various spheres of knowledge and society in relation to Islam and its fundamental principles and underlying ethos. The efforts advanced in this chapter fall within the framework pointed out above, for I will focus, in particular, on the notions of religion, secularism, and liberalism.

My basic argument is that a political order rooted in Islamic norms shares with the modern secularist orders its desire to liberate the body politics from narrow religious and cultural interpretations. Unlike the secularist order, the Islamic political order, however, encourages the fostering of moral values in accordance with the overall scheme of moral autonomy.

I conclude by emphasizing the priority of the institutions of civil society over those of the state, and the inevitability of invigorating inter-communal action to ensure the autonomy of both the individual and community, and to limit the power of the modern state.

RELIGION-POLITICS INTERPLAY

Although a deep understanding of the interaction between the political and religious spheres requires a systematic and elaborate examination of their meaning, I will limit my statement to delineating their boundaries and identifying a few areas of friction between the two.

Religion refers to those aspects of life which relate to the determination of the total meaning of existence. It is concerned, in particular, with three grand questions about human existence: its origin, its purpose, and its destiny. Although the above three questions can be raised from a philosophical point of view, the religious response to them is distinguished from the philosophical by the degree of conviction that one enjoys over the other. That is to say, a religious conclusion to these grand questions is not only supported by rational arguments, but by emotional attachment as well. This difference gives religion an advantage over philosophy in that it makes religiously based convictions a better springboard for action. It is a fact of history that people with deep religious convictions are willing to endure greater difficulties and make greater sacrifices in pursuit of their religious ideals than those whose attachment to their ideals is based on purely rational demonstration.

Paradoxically though, religion's source of strength is also its source of weakness. It is always easier to dissuade people from erroneous convictions when the latter are based on theoretical arguments rather than religious convictions. Although shared religious convictions can create more harmony in the public sphere, the possibility of interpersonal and inter-communal conflicts are bound to increase in multi-religious societies.

The question that we need to address here is not whether religion and politics stand in a conflictual or harmonious relationship, but rather how and under what conditions religious commitment can strengthen and improve the quality of social life.

DEGREES OF SECULARISM

Politics is about organizing the public sphere, that is, regulating action and deciding direction. As such, both the convictions and interests of a people influence public regulations. In its drive to develop a social order in which religion and politics strengthen one another without suppressing individuality and creativity, Europe went through two interrelated processes: religious reformation and secularization. Reformation entailed a struggle to liberate the individual from the control of religious authorities, viz. the Catholic Church. Secularization consisted of the liberation of the state from control by particular religious groups, so as to ensure that public policy was based on rational arguments, rather than religious injunctions.

However, although religion ceased to have a visible influence in the public sphere, it continued to be an important force in shaping public policy and public life. This is true because rational arguments about the nature of public order have to start from a transcendental understanding of the meaning of public life and social interaction. The notions of right and wrong, good and evil, and the tolerable and the intolerable are the result of both religious conviction and political compromise.

It is important to realize that secularization is a multi-faceted phenomenon. One facet of secularization, and the one that was initially intended by its early advocates, is the separation of State and Church. However, because it was achieved by negating history and tradition, it gradually led to the "death of God," the erosion of religious values and convictions in Western society by the turn of the twentieth century, and to the "death of man" at the dawn of the twenty-first century. The secularism of the post-modern age is ruled by the ideas of self-interest, self-indulgence, and excess.

THE ORIGIN OF SECULARISM

Secularism refers to complex and multifaceted attitudes and practices that cannot be easily captured in a brief description or rendered into a simple definition. While one may find certain similarities between modern secularist attitudes and practices and those which existed in pre-modern societies, it is fair to say that secularism as we know it today is a modern phenomenon that grew in the modern West, and later took root in different societies.

In its essential sense, secularism denotes a set of notions and values whose aim is to ensure that the state neither engages in promoting specific religious beliefs and values, nor uses its powers and offices to persecute religion. To prevent state officials from using their political authority to impose a narrow set of religious attitudes and values on the larger society, and to prevent the use of religious symbols to provoke strife among religious communities, Western intellectuals embarked on a project that aimed at separating political authority from religious affiliation. To that end, the Enlightenment scholars embraced a set of concepts and principles, and used them as the basis for reconstructing modern European consciousness. The new political ideology advanced by Enlightenment activists and thinkers emphasized concepts such as equality, freedom of conscience and conviction, and the supremacy of law, all of which were advocated by the Religious Reformation that put an end to the ancient regime of Europe.

The underlying socio-political morality advocated by the pioneers of the secular state in Europe was derived from the religious tradition delineated by the religious reformists of fifteenth-century Europe, though argued in rational terms and common-good logic. Early advocates of the separation of State and Church, such as Descartes, Hobbes, Locke, and Rousseau, had no intention of undermining religion, or faith in the Divine, but rather predicated their reformist ideas on the notion of God and civil religion. Descartes, for instance, argued: "the certainty and truth of all knowledge depends uniquely on my awareness of the true God, to such an extent that I was incapable of perfect knowledge about anything else until I became aware of him."[1] Similarly, Rousseau, while critical of the way religion was traditionally taught and practiced, recognized the need, even the necessity, of religious commitment and faith for the modern state to function properly. He therefore identified a number of "dogmas," and argued for their inclusion in the "civil religion" that he advocated:

> The existence of an omnipotent, intelligent, benevolent divinity that foresees and provides; the life to come; the happiness of the just; the punishment of sinners; the sanctity of the social contract and the law – these are the positive dogmas. As for the negative dogmas I would limit them to a single one: no intolerance.[2]

Even Kant, who limited the notion of truth to empirical experience and labored to set morality on a rational foundation, insisted that "without a God and without a world invisible to us now but hoped for, the glorious ideals of morality are indeed objects of approval and admiration, but not springs of purpose and action."[3] However, by denying the possibility of transcendental truth, and as a result of the relentless attack on the authority of revelation as a source of ethical and ontological knowledge, secularist scholars have been able to successfully marginalize religion and undermine morality. The efforts to ground morality in utility and cost-benefit calculation, rather than truth, have proved to be counter-intuitive and futile, and have given rise to egoism and moral relativism.

There were, of course, intellectuals who have less sympathy for religion, particularly among the French. Nevertheless, they did not represent the general sentiments of the great majority in Europe. Although the French revolution displayed a clear anti-religious sentiment, it was not, as Nietzsche was to discover later, directed against religion *per se,* but against organized religion, represented primarily by the Catholic Church. "Modern philosophy, being an epistemological skepticism, is," Nietzsche argued, "covertly and overtly, anti-Christian – although, to say this for the benefit of more refined ears, by no means anti-religious."[4]

The original secularist sentiment was, therefore, rooted in the religious Reformation; more specifically, it was rooted in the Protestant revolt against religious hierarchy and centralized religion. Secularism was not originally intended as a way to separate religion from society or religious consciousness from political action, but only to isolate the state from the Church structure and to separate religious and political authorities.

The tone started to change, however, a century later among progressive European intellectuals, who saw in religion a negative force whose elimination, they believed, was essential for further emancipation and progress. Karl Marx, while agreeing that the secular state had successfully neutralized religion and banished it from the public sphere, still saw a great danger in religious life. This was because, he argued, secularism reduced religion to a private matter only in so far as the state was concerned. However, the privatization of religion gave it in effect more influence in the organization of civil society. Even in the United States, where religion has been domesticated and individualized to the greatest extent, it continues to divide society into distinct religious communities, thereby allowing for the formation of internal solidarity with a clear bearing on economic life. Religion, Marx further thought, was an instrument in the hands of privileged classes to justify social misery and economic inequality. In *The Jewish Question,* Marx had the following to say about the need to emancipate humanity from religion:

> The decomposition of man into Jew and citizen, Protestant and citizen, religious man and citizen, is neither a deception directed against "citizenhood", nor is it a circumvention of political emancipation; it is political emancipation itself, the political method of emancipating oneself from religion. Of course, in periods when the political state as such is born violently out of civil society, when political liberation is the form in which men strive to achieve their liberation, the state can and must go as far as the abolition of religion, the destruction of religion. But, it can do so only in the same way that it proceeds to the abolition of private property, to the maximum, to confiscation, to progressive taxation, just as it goes as far as the abolition of life, the guillotine.[5]

Nietzsche, like Marx, condemned religion as a negative social force responsible for preserving the meek and the weak, and hence weakening the human race. By praising poverty and glorifying the taming of the natural instinct, Nietzsche insisted, religion contributed to delaying the refinement of the human species. By giving "comfort to the sufferers, courage to the oppressed and despairing, a staff and support to the dependent," Christianity, he contended, "preserved too much of what ought to perish."[6] Unlike Marx, who saw religion as an obstacle to achieving universal equality, Nietzsche's rejection of religion in general, and reformed Christianity in particular, was anti-democratic, directed against the egalitarian spirit it promoted, and hence against its failure to promote the order of rank, a hierarchical social order which he believed to be both intrinsic to humanity and desirable for social life.[7]

RELIGION AND THE STATE IN MUSLIM SOCIETY

Many Muslim intellectuals insist today that Islam is an integral part of the state. The state in a society committed to Islam, they stress, is by definition an Islamic state since political authorities are bound to Islamic Law, which has a direct bearing on constitutional law. This has created confusion about the nature of the Islamic state, and has given rise to apprehension on the part of modernist scholars, who fear that remarrying Islam and the state is bound to give birth to theocracy.

The confusion is, of course, not limited to outside observers and commentators who tend to extrapolate in their analysis from the historical experience of Western society, but also affects those who advocate the formation of a political state on the basis of Islamic values. The difficulty arises from the efforts to combine the principle of popular government with that of a state bound by the rules of Islamic Law. This confusion is, in my opinion, the result of equating the political structure of the Ummah with the political structure of the state, and consequently, confusing the functions of the Shari'ah with those of the state. This confusion is not restricted to obscure works. Rather it is found in the works of influential contemporary Islamic thinkers. In his book, *Nazariyat al-Islam wa Hadyihi*, Sayyid Abu al-Ala al-Mawdudi, for one, points out two kinds of objectives to be assigned to the Islamic state: negative objectives "like deterring the aggression and preserving the freedom of people and defending the state,"[8] and positive objectives such as "banning all forbidden things which have been condemned by the Qur'an."[9] Mawdudi concludes by affirming the totality of the state's objectives on the basis of the comprehensiveness of the Shari'ah objectives.

He writes:

> Obviously, it is impossible for such a state to limit its framework, because it is a totalitarian state encompassing the whole human life, and painting every aspect of human life with its moral color and particular reformist programs. So nobody has the right to stand up against the state and exempt himself from the liability by saying that this is a personal matter, so that the state does not intrude. In brief, the state encompasses the human life and every area of civilization according to its particular moral theory and particular reformist program. So, to some extent, it is similar to the communist and fascist state. But despite this totality the Islamic state is free from the color that dominates the totalitarian and authoritarian states of our age. Thus the Islamic state does not curtail the individual freedom nor has it much room for dictatorship or absolute authority.[10]

The above statement reflects the state of confusion that we have just pointed out. In a single paragraph the author characterizes the Islamic state as totalitarian, likens it to the communist and fascist states, and stresses that no one has the right to stand up against the state and resist its intrusion into personal life. He then contradicts himself, two sentences later, denying that the Islamic state may curtail individual freedom.

Certainly the assertion about the totalitarian character of the state is the result of mixing state functions relating to the Shari'ah's legal dimension with the functions of the Ummah concerning moral and educational dimensions. The distinction between these two kinds of objectives is, thus, of vital importance to prevent the state from imposing on the general public a normative order based on a narrow interpretation of the law. The Islamic state, it should be emphasized, is not an institution devoted to advancing the interests of the Muslim community, but a political system based on universal principles, and one committed to maintaining peace, security, and welfare for all citizens, irrespective of their doctrines, religions, nationality, race, or gender.

As will be shown below, the Islamic system in the past did not lead, nor should it lead in the future, to imposing a narrow and limited concept or a particular opinion on society. This is because the principle of religious and doctrinal plurality has been considered, since the very inception of the Ummah, a cardinal political principle. Here the Qur'anic verses, both the Makkan and Madinan, clearly stress the centrality of the principle of religious freedom in the Islamic concept.

Lately, there has been concern about the relationship between religious commitments and the exercise of power among the ranks of Islamists. Mainstream Islamic groups have been gradually moving away from the concept of a centralized Islamic political order envisaged by early leaders, such as Hassan al-Banna and Taqiyuddin al-Nabhani. Leaders of the major Islamic movements in Egypt, Jordan, Pakistan, Syria, Turkey, and Tunisia, to name a few, have come out openly in favor of a democratic, pluralistic political system, in which freedom of speech and association is guaranteed for citizens, regardless of their political orientation or religious affiliation.[11]

THE FORMATIVE PRINCIPLES
OF THE MADINAN STATE

The notion of the Islamic state advanced today by populist writers is, as I have tried to show above, a mixture of the nationalist structure of the modern state with the communal structure of historical Shari'ah. The concept of the state that emerges as a result is in complete contradiction to the nature and purpose of the polity founded by the Prophet, (ṢAAS)[12] or developed historically by successive generations of Muslims. A quick review of the guiding principles of the first Islamic polity reveals the disparity between the two. The principles and structure of the early Islamic polity are epitomized in the Covenant of Madinah (Ṣaḥīfat al-Madinah), which formed the constitutional foundation of the political community established by the Prophet.[13]

The Covenant of Madinah established a number of important political principles that, put together, formed the political constitution of the first Islamic state, and defined the political rights and duties of the members of the newly established political community, Muslims and non-Muslims alike, and drew up the political structure of the nascent society. The most important principles included in this Covenant are as follows:

1. The Covenant declared that the Ummah is a political society, open to all individuals committed to its principles and values, and ready to shoulder its burdens and responsibilities. It is not an exclusive society, whose membership rights and security are restricted to a select few. The right to membership of the Ummah is specified in: (a) accepting the principles of the Islamic system, manifested in the commitment to adhere to the moral and legal order; and (b) declaring allegiance to the system by practical contributions and struggle to actualize the objectives and goals of Islam. Thus, allegiance and concern for public good are the principles determining the membership of the Ummah as defined by the first article of the document: "This is a Covenant offered by Muhammad the Prophet, [governing the relations] among the believers and the Muslims of Quraysh and Yathrib [Madinah], and those who followed, joined, and labored with them."[14]

2. The Covenant delineated a general framework that defined individual norms and the scope of political action within the new society, but preserved the basic social and political structures prevalent then in tribal Arabia. The Covenant of Madinah preserved tribal structure, while negating tribal spirit and subordinating tribal allegiance to a morally based legal order. Since the Covenant declared that the nascent political community is "an Ummah to the exclusion of all people," it approved a tribal division that had already been purged of the tribal spirit epitomized by the slogan "my brethren right or wrong," subjecting it to the higher principles of truth and justice. The Covenant therefore

declared that the emigrants of the Quraysh, Banū al-Ḥārith, Banū al-'Aws, and other tribes residing in Madinah, according "to their present customs, shall pay the blood wit they paid previously and that every group shall redeem its prisoners."[15]

Islam's avoidance of the elimination of tribal divisions can be explained by a number of factors that can be summarized in the following three points:

(a) The tribal division was not based merely on politics but also social differentiation, thus providing its people with a symbiotic system. Therefore, the abolition of the political and social assistance provided by the tribe before developing an alternative would have been a great loss to the people affected.

(b) Apart from its being a social division, the tribe represented an economic division in harmony with the pastoral economy prevalent in the Arabian Peninsula before and after Islam. The tribal division is the ideal basis of pastoral production, for it provides freedom of movement and migration in search of pasture. Any change in this pattern requires taking the initiative to change the means and methods of production.

(c) Perhaps the most important factor that justified the tribal division within the framework of the Ummah after the final Message had purged the tribal character of its aggression and arrogance, is the maintenance of the society and its protection from the danger of central dictatorship. Such a situation might arise in the absence of a secondary social and political structure and the concentration of political power in the hands of a central authority.

Hence Islam adopted a political system, based on the concept of the one Ummah, as an alternative to the divisional tribal system, while upholding the tribal division now cleansed of its aggressive elements. Islam left the question of changing the political structure to the gradual development of economic and production structures. Although Islamic Revelation avoided any arbitrary directives aimed at immediate abolition of the tribal division, it criticized openly tribal and nomadic life.[16]

3. The Islamic political system adopted the principle of religious tolerance based on the freedom of belief for all the members of society. It conceded to the Jews the right to act according to the principles and

rulings in which they believed: "The Jews of Banū ʿAwf are one community with the believers. The Jews have their religion and the
Muslims theirs." The Covenant emphasized the fundamentality of
cooperation between Muslims and non-Muslims in establishing justice
and defending Madinah against foreign aggression. "The Jews must
bear their expenses and the Muslims their expenses. Each must help the
other against anyone who attacks the people of this Covenant. They
must seek mutual advice and consultation." It prohibited the Muslims
from doing injustice to the Jews or seeking revenge for their Muslim
brothers against the followers of the Jewish religion without adhering
to the principles of truth and goodness. "To the Jew who follows us
belong help and equality. He shall not be wronged nor shall his enemies
be aided."[17]

4. The Covenant stipulated that the social and political activities in the
   new system must be subject to a set of universal values and standards
   that treat all people equally. Sovereignty in the society would not rest
   with the rulers or any particular group, but with the law founded on the
   basis of justice and goodness, maintaining the dignity of all. The
   Covenant emphasized repeatedly and frequently the fundamentality of
   justice, goodness, and righteousness, and used various expressions to
   condemn injustice and tyranny. "They would redeem their prisoners
   with kindness and justice common among the believers," the Covenant
   stated. "The God-conscious believers shall be against the rebellious,
   and against those who seek to spread injustice, sin, enmity, or corruption among the believers; the hand of every person shall be against him,
   even if he be a son of one of them," it proclaimed.[18]

5. The Covenant introduced a number of political rights to be enjoyed by
   the individuals of the Madinan State, Muslims and non-Muslims alike,
   such as (a) the obligation to help the oppressed, (b) outlawing guilt by
   association, which was commonly practiced by pre-Islamic Arab
   tribes: "A person is not liable for his ally's misdeeds;" (c) freedom of
   belief: "The Jews have their religion and the Muslims have theirs;" and
   (d) freedom of movement from and to Madinah: "Whoever leaves is
   safe, and whoever stays in Madinah is safe except those who have
   wronged [others], or committed sin."[19]

RELIGION AND THE STATE
IN HISTORICAL MUSLIM SOCIETY

Adhering to the guidance of Revelation, the Ummah respected the principle of religious plurality and cultural diversity during most of its long history. The successive governments since the *Rāshidūn* period preserved the freedom of faith and allowed non-Muslim minorities not only to practice their religious rituals and proclaim their beliefs, but also to implement their religious laws according to an autonomous administrative system. Likewise, the Ummah as a whole respected the doctrinal plurality with both its conceptual and legal dimensions. It resisted every attempt to draw the political power into taking sides with partisan groups, or into preferring one ideological group to another. It also insisted on reducing the role of the state and restricting its functions to a limited sphere.

Anyone who undertakes to study the political history of Islam will soon realize that all the political practices which violated the principle of religious freedom and plurality were an exception to the rule. For instance, the efforts of the Caliph al-Maʿmūn to impose doctrinal uniformity in accordance with the Muʿtazili interpretations, and to use his political authority to support one of the parties to the doctrinal disputes, were condemned by the ʿalims and the majority of the Ummah. His efforts to achieve doctrinal homogeneity by suppression and force eventually clashed with the will of the Ummah, which refused to solve doctrinal and theoretical problems by the sword. This compelled al-Wāthiq Billāh, the third Caliph after al-Maʿmūn to give up the role assumed by his predecessors and abandon their oppressive measures.

Obviously, Muslims have historically recognized that the main objective of establishing a political system is to create the general conditions that allow the people to realize their duties as moral agents of the Divine will (*Khulafā'*), not to impose the teachings of Islam by force. We therefore ascribe the emergence of organizations which aim to compel the Ummah to follow a narrow interpretation, and which call for the use of the political power to make people obedient to the Islamic norms, to the habit of confusing the role and objectives of the Ummah with the role and objectives of the state. The Ummah aims to build Islamic identity, to provide an atmosphere conducive to the spiritual and mental development of the individual, and to grant him or her the opportunity to fulfill his or her role in life within the general framework of the law. Meanwhile, the state makes the effort to coordinate the Ummah's activities so as to employ the natural and human potential and possibilities to overcome the political and economic problems and obstacles that hinder the Ummah's development.

Differentiating between the general and particular in the Shariʿah and between the responsibilities of the Ummah and the state, is a necessity if we want to avoid the transformation of political power into a device for advancing particular interests. We must also ensure that state agencies and institutions do not arrest intellectual and social progress, nor obstruct the spiritual, conceptual, and organizational developments of society.

DIFFERENTIATING CIVIL SOCIETY AND THE STATE

Historically, legislative functions in Muslim society were not restricted to state institutions. Rather, there was a wide range of legislation related to juristic efforts at both the moral and legal levels. Since the major part of legislation relating to transactional and contractual relations among individuals is attached to the juristic legislative bodies, the judicial tasks may be connected directly with the Ummah, not with the state. It must be emphasized that the differentiation between civil society and the state can be maintained only by dividing legislation into distinct areas that reflect both the geographical and normative differentiation of the political society.

The importance of the differential structure of the law is not limited to its ability to counteract the tendency to centralize power, which characterizes the Western model of the state. Rather, it is also related to guarantees extended to religious minorities. The Islamic model should maintain the legislative and administrative independence of the followers of different religions, for the sphere of communal legislation does not fall under the governmental authority of the state. On the other hand, the majoritarian model of the democratic state deprives religious minorities of their legal independence, and insists on subjugating all citizens to a single legal system, which often reflects the doctrinal and behavioral values of the ruling majority.

The early Muslim community was cognizant of the need to differentiate law to ensure moral autonomy, while working diligently to ensure equal protection by the law of fundamental human rights. Thus early jurists recognized that non-Muslims who have entered into a peace covenant with Muslims are entitled to full religious freedom and equal protection by the law of their rights to personal safety and property. Muḥammad ibn al-Ḥasan al-Shaybānī states in unequivocal terms that when non-Muslims enter into a peace covenant with Muslims,

> Muslims should not appropriate any of their [the non-Muslims'] houses and land, nor should they intrude into any of their dwellings. [This is because they have become party to a covenant of peace, and because on the day of [the peace of] Khaybar, the Prophet's spokesman announced that none of the property of the covenanter is permitted to them [the Muslims]. [It is also because they [the non-Muslims] have accepted the peace covenant so as they may enjoy their properties and rights on a par with the Muslims.[20]

Similarly, early Muslim jurists recognized the right of non-Muslims to self-determination, and awarded them full moral and legal autonomy in the villages and towns under their control. Therefore, al-Shaybānī, the author of the most authoritative work on non-Muslim rights, insisted that the Christians who entered into a peace covenant (*dhimma*) – hence became *dhimmis* – had all the freedom to trade in wine and pork in their towns, even though this practice was considered immoral and illegal among Muslims.[21] However, *dhimmis* were prohibited to do the same in towns and villages controlled by Muslims.

Likewise, early Muslim jurists recognized the right of *dhimmis* to hold public office, including that of a judge or a minister. However, because judges had to refer to laws sanctioned by the religious traditions of the various religious communities, non-Muslim judges could not administer law in Muslim communities, nor were Muslim judges permitted to enforce Shariʿah laws on the *dhimmis*. There was no disagreement among the various schools of jurisprudence on the right of non-Muslims to be ruled according to their laws; they differed only over whether the positions held by non-Muslim magistrates were judicial in nature, and hence the magistrates could be called judges, or whether they were purely political, and therefore the magistrates were indeed political leaders.[22] Al-Māwardī hence distinguished between two types of ministerial positions: *plenipotentiary* minister (*wazīr tafwīḍ*) and executive minister (*wazīr tanfīdh*). The two positions differed in that the former acted independently from the Caliph, while the latter had to act on the instructions of the Caliph, and within the limitations set by him.[23] Therefore, early jurists permitted *dhimmis* to hold the office of the executive, but not that of the *plenipoten-tiary* minister.[24]

However, while early Shariʿah Law recognized the civil and political rights and liberties of non-Muslim *dhimmis*, its rules underwent drastic revision, beginning in the eighth century AH. This was a time of great political turmoil throughout the Muslim world. It was during that time that the Mongols invaded Central and West Asia, inflicting tremendous losses on various dynasties and kingdoms, and destroying the seat of the Caliphate in Baghdad. This coincided with the Crusaders' control of Palestine and the coast of Syria. In the West, the Muslim power in Spain was being gradually eroded. It was under such conditions of mistrust and suspicion that a set of provisions attributed to an agreement between the Caliph ʿUmar and the Syrian Christians were publicized in a treatise written by Ibn al-Qayyim.[25] Although the origin of these provisions is dubious, their intent is clear: to humiliate Christian *dhimmis* and to set them apart in dress code and appearance. Their impact, however, was limited, for the Ottomans, who replaced the Abbasids as the hegemonic power in the Muslim world, continued the early practice of granting legal and administrative autonomy to non-Muslim subjects.

ISLAM, CIVIL SOCIETY, AND THE STATE

The modern state emerged to foster individual freedom from arbitrary rule, and to ensure that the members of the political society assumed full control over public institutions. To do so, the modern state found it necessary to free public institutions from the control of all exclusive groups, including organized religions. However, despite the clear desire of the pioneers of the secular state to replace religious morality with civic virtue as the moral foundation of the state, secularism gradually developed antireligious tendencies, leading to the steady erosion of the moral consensus. The continual erosion of morality and the rampant corruption in modern politics threatens to turn the state into an instrument in the hands of corrupt officials and their egoistic cronies.

This has prompted calls for the return of religion and religiously organized groups into the political arena. Nowhere are these calls louder and clearer than in Muslim societies where Islamic values have historically exerted great influence on the body politic. Unfortunately, the reunion envisaged by the advocates of the Islamic state is often presented in crude and simplistic terms, for it fails to appreciate the great care that was taken by the early Muslims to ensure that the state incorporated, both in its objectives and structure, the freedom and interest of all intra- and inter-religious divisions.

This calls upon Muslim scholars to engage in new thinking that aims at redefining political principles and authority. In doing so, Muslim scholars should be fully aware of the need to transcend the historical models of political organizations in Muslim society. Political structures and proce-dures adopted by early Muslim societies are directly linked to their social structures, economic and technological developments, and political expe-riences. While historical Islamic models provide a mine of knowledge for contemporary Muslims to utilize, any workable formulation of the mod-ern Islamic model of the state that is true to Islamic values and ethos must emerge from fresh thinking that takes into account the structure of mod-ern society.

Islamic political thought, I believe, can make a profound significant contribution toward reclaiming the moral core of social life and preserving religious traditions, without sacrificing the principle of freedom and equal-ity promoted by the modern state. The hallmark of Islamic political ex-perience is the limitations that historical Muslim society was able to place on the actions of rulers, and the presence of a vigorous and robust civil soci-ety. Many of the functions that the secular state assumes today were en-trusted to civic institutions, including education, health, and legislation. The state was mainly entrusted with questions of security and defense, and was the last resort in questions relating to dispensation of justice. This understanding of state power would potentially free religious communities from intervention by the state and state officials, who tend to enforce their religiously based values and notions on the members of society, including those who do not share with them some of those values and beliefs.

The notions of individual freedom and equality are intrinsic to Islamic political thought, and those principles require that individuals have the basic civil liberties offered by the modern state. However, by freeing civil society from the heavy hand of the state, and by extending individual liberties to the community and recognizing the moral autonomy of social groups, social and religious groups under the Islamic conception of law (Shariʿah) would have the capacity to legislate their internal morality and affairs in their communities. While the new sphere of freedom acquired under this arrangement would allow for differentiation among citizens, equality would have to be maintained as the criterion of justice in the new area of public law, and in access to public institutions – that is, in matters relating to shared interests and inter-communal relations.

3

Al-Māwardī's Political Paradigm: Principles of the Islamic Political System

SYED A. AHSANI

FOLLOWING THE WESTERN domination of Muslim countries, Islamic thinkers have reacted to it on three levels in respect of its political system. First, the apologists have advocated the total adoption of the Western model of democracy. In reaction, the traditionalists argue that the wholesale adoption of the Western model will lead to secularization, contradicting the Islamic value system. The third group, the moderates, take the middle of the road position – benefiting from Western learning as the lost heritage of Islam, but also observing the fundamentals of Islamic Sharīʿah. These divisions are not new; they existed in the Abbasid period when the Muʿtazilites (the rationalists) gave primacy to reason. The rise of philosophy under Caliph al-Maʾmūn inspired the fear that Revelation might be threatened by Reason, which provoked two kinds of reaction: *Ahl al-Ḥadīth* or the traditionalists, who totally rejected reason; and the Ashʿarites, who put limits on it in order to save Revelation from being rejected. Māwardī, who took up the debate in later times when the rationalists had been banned, was neither *Ahl al-Ḥadīth* nor Ashʿarite, but an independent thinker who held firmly to rationalist theology, where Revelation was silent, and did not lay down the law. His greatest contribution was the introduction of the concept of "political justice" into the Sharīʿah.

Māwardī's *al-Aḥkām al-Sulṭāniyyah* laid down the public law in such a manner that it deemed Sharīʿah an insufficient yardstick for *ʿadl* (justice).

This points to the developed practice among Muslim rulers of defining the Shariʿah as the observance of religion in line with the recommendations of the ʿalims. This practice satisfied the ʿalims, who then undertook to abstain from judging the politics of the Caliph. Interestingly, this led to the separation of religion from politics, indirectly defeating the commonly held view that the secular and the religious are inseparable in Islam.[1] The root of this idea lay in the practice of Prophet Muhammad – as Prophet and Statesman – and *al-Khulafāʾ al-Rāshidūn,* in the formative period of Islam.[2]

THE CONSTITUTION OF MADINAH

The Madinah state was the oldest known in history; it established the principle of legality, that is, submission of the state to the rule of law.

THE SALIENT FEATURES OF THE CONSTITUTION OF MADINAH

1. The territory became the basis for granting citizenship instead of tribal lineage. All residents became one community, including polytheists and the Jews (Articles 20b and 25).

2. The Prophet became the Head of State and the Final Court of Appeal.

3. The practice of tyranny and injustice was rejected (Articles 13, 15, 16, 36 and 47). Equality was established as the basic principle of an Islamic state (Articles 15, 17, 19 and 45).

4. The principle of *pacta sunt servanda* [treaties are binding], as laid down in modern international law, was adopted, allowing other tribes and minorities to accede to the Madinah Charter.

5. Specific provisions were made regarding murder, the sheltering of criminals, liability of only those who committed crimes, and the preclusion of individuals from signing separate peace with enemies of the state. The Jews were allowed a share in the booty and also a share in the expenses of war. In that case, they did not pay the *jizyah* (poll tax).

6. Some traditions like blood money were maintained on the principle of ʿurf (customary law), preserving what was sound and abolishing what was corrupt.

7. The Constitution was a comprehensive document, covering all the exigencies: jurisprudence, defense, plans for raids and battles if attacked, financial resources, zakah, treaties, and delegations.

8. The political system established by the Constitution of Madinah covered the functions of Legislature,[3] Judiciary and Executive, anticipating the modern state system.[4]

While studying the Māwardī paradigm in the context of Muʿtazilite and Asha'rite debates, an attempt will be made to delineate the principles that we can learn and adopt from al-Khulafa' al-Rāshidūn (Rightly Guided Caliphs) model. Also, this chapter will seek to underline the principles of an Islamic state. After this analysis of past practices, especially in the light of the Qur'an and Sunnah, it can be determined as to how far the present democratic model is in consonance with the Islamic political system, based on the Qur'an and Sunnah. If it is not, what model can be evolved and adopted on the basis of ijtihad[5] in light of the evolution of modern political thought over the centuries, not only in the Muslim world but in the West as well?

DISTINCTIVE FEATURES
OF ISLAMIC POLITICAL THEORY

Upon the death of the Prophet, the Anṣār gathered, and three Muhajirūn Companions joined them (Abū Bakr, ʿUmar, and ʿUbaydah ibn al-Jarrāḥ) at Banī Saqīfah where Abū Bakr was elected Caliph of the Messenger – Khalīfat al-Rasūl.[6] Later, this election was confirmed by voting bayʿah (handshake) in the General Assembly at the Madinah Mosque. The following principles were established at Banī Saqīfah, as part of the political theory of Islam:

1. The election of the Caliph was to be by Shūrā (consultation), in two stages, indicating that it was for the Muslims to decide, since the Prophet did not take any decision on the matter, leaving it to the

community to decide, given the time and the place. The will of the community was, therefore, an essential principle for selecting the Head of State as successor to the Prophet – *Khalīfat al-Rasūl*. ʿUmar, who became the Second Caliph, later told the Council of Elders, meaning the elders with knowledge, wisdom, and discernment (*ahl al-ḥal wa al-ʿaqd* [those who loosen and bind]): "You must kill any one of you who claims command over you without consulting the Muslims."[7] The method of consultation is not prescribed in the Qur'an and Traditions, and can vary depending on the time and circumstances, as is evident from the election of the four Rightly Guided Caliphs.[8]

2. The criterion for electing a Head of State is excellence in religion, *taqwā*. However, a Caliph is also the temporal Head of State,[9] as has been described in detail by Māwardī in *al-Aḥkām al-Sultāniyyah*.[10]

3. The selection of a Caliph cannot brook any delay, even for the burial of the Prophet.[11] The Companions did not want to be without a *jamāʿah* even for part of the day.[12]

However, ʿUmar was nominated by Abū Bakr, with the consultation of *ahl al-ḥal wa al-ʿaqd*. According to Māwardī, this was election by a single elector, a precedent quoted by later jurisconsults in justification of the nomination of sons by Caliphs and sultans. However, Māwardī failed to mention this practice as something in violation of the essential criteria of religious knowledge, ijtihad, judgment, courage, and physical health, apart from the Caliph being a member of the Quraysh.

The selection of ʿUmar, tantamount to an election which he was bound to win in general voting or *bayʿah,* was fully justified in the light of his vast knowledge, administrative judgment, and great services to Islam during the Prophet's time, and as a close Adviser to Abū Bakr, the first Caliph.

The election of ʿUthmān established the principle that the office of the Caliphate was not hereditary, for ʿUmar, unable to make a choice while selecting the Electoral College omitted his son, ʿAbdullāh, on the grounds of being his son. Also, it established the precedent that six persons could constitute an Electoral College, while other jurists considered three, or even one, sufficient, as was the case in ʿAbbās's *bayʿah* [handshake] of ʿAlī, who was told that if he did not accept, the rebels against ʿUthmān could elect one of their own. Besides, ʿAlī was one of the six candidates considered by ʿUmar to fulfill the conditions for the office of Caliphate. After the third Caliph ʿUthmān's assassination, he was the only choice.

The assassination of ʿUthmān raised the issue of rebellion against the Caliph, whether it is justified in Islamic political theory. Most jurisconsults view it as unwarranted on the basis of a Tradition:

> After me governors will rule over you, and those who are upright will rule over you with their uprightness, and those who are corrupt will rule over you with their corruption; listen to them and obey them in everything which is compatible with truth – if they are correct in their dealings, then it will be to your benefit and theirs, and if they act incorrectly, then that will still be to your benefit [in the next world] but will be held against them.[13]

Rebellion is justified in the case of "unbelief" as provided in the Qur'an. Al-Ḥasan al-Baṣrī, a leading *tabiʿī* (second generation Companion), prohibited fighting against the ruler in a civil war. Learning and practicing Islam was better than arguing and bickering, so said some scholars who refrained from rebellion against the ruler, for it would lead to chaos and anarchy, far more harmful than tyrannical rule despite its long duration. A well-known *fiqhī* doctrine says: "When you are faced with two damaging situations, choose the lesser evil."[14] Those who justify rebellion against the ruler rely on Abū Bakr's sermon on his election: "Follow me if I am acting according to the Qur'an and Sunnah, but do not obey me if I do otherwise."[15]

Accordingly, some who were influenced by the propaganda of a converted Jew, ʿAbdullah ibn Saba', came from Iraq and Egypt to Madinah, demanding ʿUthmān's resignation despite his clarification in response to their accusations of nepotism in appointing his relatives as Governors.[16]

According to Rashid Riḍa, the Imamate of Necessity, *imāmat al-ḍarūrah*, must be obeyed while fulfilling its raison d'être of justice, efficiency, and descent from Quraysh (though Kharijites, Ibn Khaldūn and Ottomans disagreed) in order to avoid anarchy and chaos. However, rebellion is justified on grounds of the Caliph's loss of moral probity, physical disability, insanity, captivity, apostasy, disbelief, or injustice. Therefore, *ahl al-ḥal wa al-ʿaqd*, should resist oppression, but the urge to revolt must be weighed against the fear that it might result in anarchy, which Islam seeks to avoid

as far as possible. Al-Ghazālī, Ibn Taymiyyah considered quietism or submission to injustice preferable to anarchy incidental to rebellion. It is said:
"The status quo, being the lesser of the two evils, is preferable to civil
strife." Nevertheless, the Turks revolted against the Ottoman Sultans
in 1924. In opposing rebellion, Rashid Riḍa agrees with Ibn Taymiyyah,
who made Muslims conscious of a forced choice between anarchy and
injustice.[17]

Traditionally, the ʿalims were defenders and monitors of the status
quo. As *ahl al-ḥal wa al-ʿaqd*, they were expected to oversee that the ruler
enforced the Shariʿah, assuming responsibility for proper management of
public affairs and restoring the pristine standards of simplicity, humility,
and frugality in lifestyle. Also, they were to ensure that those who wanted
to occupy the office might be debarred in accordance with a tradition:
"*ṭālib al-wilayah lā yuwallā*" a seeker of office should not be given it.[18]

Some of these principles for the election of the Caliph are: *shūrā*, justice, freedom, equality, succession, and election. The Islamic political
system does not lay down specific and detailed system of governance. It is
be more correct to say that the Shariʿah delineates general principles only,
leaving further details to specific circumstances of time and place. The
Caliph who is elected should enjoy sound health, possess knowledge of the
Shariʿah to exercise ijtihad, and be able to implement domestic and foreign
policy with ability, courage, and wisdom. He should abide by the Shariʿah
and promote public good. So long as he does this, Muslims should obey
him, offer him advice on what is right, and correct him if he is wrong. The
principle of *shūrā* was followed by the four Rightly-Guided Caliphs in
four different ways, proving that changes in circumstances can result in the
adoption of a different methodology.[19]

SHŪRĀ (CONSULTATION)

Shūrā is the most important principle of Islamic political theory. Addres-
sing the Prophet, the Qur'an informed him:

> It is by the mercy of Allah that you were lenient with them, for if you had
> been rough and harsh-hearted, they would have dispersed from around
> you. So pardon them and ask forgiveness for them and consult with them
> on the matter. (3:159)

In order to underline the importance of *Shūrā*, Allah is directing the

Prophet to consult with them despite their view being contrary to the Prophet's, who was in favor of fighting the infidels within the confines of Madinah while the Companions advised going out. He was proved right, but since he accepted their advice, the Companions were absolved of their error of judgment. Also, it indicates that the leader should not bear a grudge for giving the wrong advice, nor refrain from future consultation. Further, the Qur'an says:

> And those who answer the call of their Lord and establish prayer and who conduct their affairs by counsel, and who spend of what We have bestowed upon them. (42:38)

According to Shaykh Muhammad Abdu, *shūrā* is mandatory, for consultation is an essential quality of those who "enjoin good and forbid wrong." Abū Hurayrah said, "I have never seen anyone else who seeks consultation of his Companions more than the Prophet himself." However, *Shūrā* is not required where there is revelation, though the Prophet held *Shūrā* even though *Waḥi* had come as in the case of the Treaty of Ḥudaybiyyah. However, *Shūrā* was also extended to the interpretation of the Divine Revelation and matters in which there was no *Waḥi*[20].[21]

When asking for *Shūrā* (Advice), the ruler should not dismiss or veto the advice, for the Prophet followed the advice of the Companions for going out in ʿUḥud. *Bayʿah* or the oath of fealty is conditional upon the Caliph abiding by the *Shūrā*, otherwise *Bayʿah* becomes null and void. This view is held by the majority of jurisconsults. Their minority which consider *Shūrā* not binding rely on the verse: "When you decide, put your trust in Allah" (3:159), apart from the Sunnah of the Prophet in Ḥudaybiyyah; Abū Bakr's stand in sending an army to Syria; his waging war against the apostates; and ʿUmar's decision not to distribute lands occupied in Iraq, but retain them for future generations. Ṭabarī considers the above-mentioned verse relevant to *Waḥi* (Revelation), which must be followed irrespective of the *Shūrā*, as happened in Ḥudaybiyyah. Then ʿUmar's inquiry from the Prophet as to why Muslims should accept the peace was 'Naṣīḥah' and not *Shūrā*, and before he was told by the Prophet about *Waḥi*. Though not obligatory, Abū Bakr's holding *Shūrā* in following the Prophet's action of dispatching the army to Syria, was indicative of the imperative nature of *Shūrā*, laying a precedent for future generations, proving at the same time that even though not abiding by *Shūrā* advice, he had carried out *Shūrā*, in form and spirit, for they, including ʿUmar, promptly reconsidered their opinion, agreeing to Abū Bakr's reasoning.

Likewise, ʿUmar was able to win the *Shūrā* over his decision on land in Iraq. Indeed, *Shūrā* is mandatory on both the ruler and the ruled as a religious duty, *ʿibādah*: on the ruler to hold *Shūrā*, and on the ruled to give the right advice. If a ruler does not hold *Shūrā* and the ruled do not offer advice, they are guilty of dereliction of religious obligation, committing a sin.

Where there is no *Waḥi*, *Shūrā* is to be held at three levels:

1. *Ahl al-ḥal wa al-ʿaqd* as practiced by the Prophet and the Rightly Guided Caliphs.

2. Specialists who have an advanced level of knowledge on the subject such as war, foreign policy, or domestic policy, etc.

3. Referendum/Parliament/Popular Vote.

It is exercised where *Shūrā* of *ahl al-ḥal wa al-ʿaqd* has been held and the decision is put before the people for ratification. During the time of the Prophet or the Rightly Guided Caliphs, there was no permanent *Majlis*, Cabinet, or Parliament. A vote was not held, nor was there a formal majority/minority, or government in power and party in Opposition. The *Shūrā* proceedings were confidential and *Shūrā* members did not publicize their opinions, leaving the announcement to the ruler, who had direct access to the people without *ahl al-ḥal wa al-ʿaqd* acting as the spokespersons.

Also, once *Shūrā* was given, the Wise Elders did not feel let down if their opinion was not accepted. The *Shūrā* was given with a good intention, regardless of personal ego or gaining benefit. In fact, *Shūrā* was an exercise in ijtihad, which aimed at finding the truth with due concentration on an effort by people gifted with the knowledge of the Shariʿah and right judgment.

SOME EXAMPLES OF *SHŪRĀ* BY THE PROPHET

Before Badr: On receiving the news that a trade caravan of Quraysh was proceeding to Syria, the Prophet held a *Shūrā* (consultation) about pursuing it, not engaging in a fight. The Companions, the majority of whom were *Anṣārs* (Madinah Helpers), pledged full support, unlike the Bani

Israel, who had asked Moses to go and fight. The Prophet went with the Companions in pursuit, making the departure public as a strategy, with the result that Abū Sufyān asked for reinforcements from Makkah and changed the route via the coast. A second *Shūrā* was held to decide whether to return to Madinah or confront the reinforcements coming from Makkah. In Madinah, there was a distinct possibility of the hypocrites, the Bedouins, the non-Muslim Arabs, and the Jews taking advantage of the absence of Muslims. Also, they came hardly prepared for a regular battle, numbering only 313. Nonetheless, they again pledged full support to proceed to Badr. Meanwhile, the Prophet received the revelation that Muslims preferred to go after booty whereas Allah had destined victory for them. His action to seek advice was to reinforce the Companions' conviction and enthusiasm.[22]

The lesson is that the leader should not disclose his own personal judgment before allowing the free expression of other opinions. The Prophet decided to camp in a low area. Munzir, a Companion, finding that it was not the result of revelation, advised occupying a spring on high ground to deprive the Quraysh any access to water; it was not a *Shūrā*, but 'Naṣīḥah', given privately, indicating that one should not hesitate to express one's opinion to the Commander, who should carefully consider it and accept any sound and timely advice from anyone regardless of one's status. This was done by the Prophet, who announced the decision without any public disclosure as to who had made the suggestion influencing it.[23]

Before the fight, the Prophet announced that ʿAbbās and another Companion should not be killed; Abū Ḥudhaifah disagreed, vowing to kill him. The Prophet asked ʿUmar, who had known of ʿAbbās's secret conversion to Islam, whether hurting ʿAbbās made sense. ʿUmar offered to kill Ḥudhayfah, but was restrained by the Prophet, who, realizing that Abū Ḥudhayfah's vow reflected ignorance, excused him, thus establishing the Sunnah principle that a commander should tolerate free expression and difference of opinion for which he should not punish the dissenter.

After Badr: The Prophet held *Shūrā* about the prisoners of war. Abū Bakr advised accepting *fidyah*, whereas ʿUmar and four other Companions favored killing them. The Prophet went inside to reflect and on coming out, he favored the suggestion of Abū Bakr, who also knew about ʿAbbās's conversion to Islam. The Prophet's similitude to Abū Bakr as Jesus, saying "some are softer than milk," and ʿUmar's similitude to Noah, "others are harder than stone," show that there is room for both traits of human nature.[24]

Here, the Prophet, knowing the supreme national interest and helped by *Waḥi* (Revelation), not by self-interest, did not disclose it so as to allow free expression of opinions. He did not oppose any opinion outright without full reflection on it. This establishes the principle of Islamic political theory that *Shūrā* is mandatory, on both the ruler and the ruled. This *Shūrā* on prisoners of war also lays down the principle for the ruler that it is Sunnah (the Prophetic example) to keep the counsel or private judgment confidential to oneself so as not to stifle free expression. That is why Allah in His Infinite Mercy supported the consensus[25] "*yadu Allah maʿa al-jamaʿah*"; He asked the Prophet to forgive those in favor of *fidyah*.[26]

JUSTICE

Justice is the cardinal principle of Islam:

> Allah enjoins justice and kindness, and charity to kin, and forbids indecency and abomination, and wickedness. (16:90)

> Allah orders you that you return the trust to their rightful owners, and that if you judge between people, you judge justly. (4:58)

> And do not let hatred of any people dissuade you from dealing justly. Deal justly, for that is closer to Godliness. (5:8)

> O you who believe! Be firm in justice as witness for Allah, even in such cases as are against yourselves, your parents or your kin. (4:135)

> And if you give your word, you must be just, even though it be against your kin, and fulfill the covenant of Allah. For that is what He has commanded you so that you may remember. (6:152)

> Verily, We have sent Our Messengers with clear Signs, and revealed with them the Book and the Scale of [judgment] so that people may be firm in Justice; and We provided iron, wherein is mighty power and many uses for mankind, and that Allah shall know who will help Him and His Messengers in the unseen. (57:25)

Ibn Taymiyyah said:

> The aim of commissioning the prophets and of revealing the Books, there-fore, is to have people administer Justice in the cause of Allah and in the right of His creatures ... Thus he who deviates from the Book shall be cor-rected by iron [force of arms].[27]

Ibn Taymiyyah also stated: "Allah gives victory to a non-Muslim Government which is just and defeats the Muslim government which oppresses."[28]

> The indictment shall be upon those who oppress people, and those who commit injustice and wrongdoing on earth shall be severely punished. (42:42)

> Allah does not like that evil be spoken about openly except by one who has been wronged. (4:148)

> Those who are fighting have been granted permission to do so because they have been oppressed, and Allah is indeed able to grant them victory. (22:39)

> And those towns which We destroyed when they became oppressors, and We had set a fixed time for their destruction. (18:59)

> And those who commit oppression shall know what kind of destiny they shall meet. (26:227)

According to the hadiths (the Prophet's Traditions), "the just ruler will be placed foremost among the seven whom Allah will cover with His Shade on the Day when there will be no shade but His."[29] The Prophet warned: "Stay clear of oppression, for oppression is darkness on the Day of Judgment."[30]

FREEDOM

Freedom is another principle of the Islamic political system. To protect their freedom of belief and expression, Muslims should migrate to a coun-try where they can worship Allah and carry out their religious obligations. The migration of the early Muslims to Abyssinia set a precedent.

The Abyssinia migration proves that those people who consider migration to the United States or any other non-Muslim country to be a sin have not understood the Qur'an and Sunnah. On the Day of Judgment, Allah will ask Muslims who were persecuted in their homeland whether the earth was not wide enough for migration. This concept is further supported by the Prophetic mission assigned to Muslims – al-ʿamr bi al-Maʿrūf wa al-nahī ʿan al-Munkar (to enjoin good and forbid evil,) which allows freedom of opinion and expression. Muslims should have the freedom to say whether they consider an act to be: permissible (Mubāḥ) or obligatory (Wājib). Under Mubāḥ, a Muslim has the choice to do it or ignore it, as distinct from Wājib, "what is required to be done", to the extent that neglecting it is a sin. The exercise of the right to "enjoin good and forbid evil" has broad applications, covering all aspects of public life, be they political, economic, or social.

EQUALITY

Long before the American Bill of Rights and Rousseau's Social Contract established the principle of equality, the Qur'an said:

> O people! We have created you from a male and female, and have made you nations and tribes so that you may know each other. Verily the most honored of you in the sight of Allah is [the one who is] the most righteous of you. And Allah is the Knower, Aware. (49:13)

The Prophet said: "Allah has relieved you of the fanaticism of Jāhiliyyah and its pride in ancestors. Whether you are a pious Muslim or a miserable debauchee, you are the son of Adam and Adam was [made] from dust."[31]

Again, in his farewell message, he said:

> Indeed, there is no superiority of an Arab over a non-Arab, and indeed, no superiority of a red man over a black one except in Taqwā [fear or consciousness of Allah]. However, before the Law, everybody is equal, pious or impious; the pious will receive the reward in the Hereafter.[32]

When a Companion intervened on behalf of a noblewoman who had committed robbery, the Prophet said: "By Allah, if Fāṭimah, the daughter of Muhammad had committed theft, I would have had her hands cut off." Caliph Abū Bakr said in his first address after assuming office: "And the weak among you shall be strong in my eyes until I secure his right, and the strong shall be weak in my eyes until I wrest the right from him."

Once ʿAlī, the fourth Caliph, appeared before a judge as a defendant against a Jew who allegedly stole his armor. When the judge asked him to sit next to him, he reminded the judge that his preferential treatment was a violation of the principle of equality between the complainant and the defendant. The judge refused to accept the evidence of Ḥasan on the grounds that he was ʿAlī's son, allowing the Jew to retain the armor, whereupon the Jew, impressed by the impartial justice of an independent judiciary, became a Muslim.

ACCOUNTABILITY OF THE HEAD OF STATE

As the ruled are to obey the ruler who can use force to quell their rebellion, the ruled has the right to question the ruler when he abuses his authority. The Qur'an says: "And when he turns away, he will try to spread corruption on earth and to destroy the crops and mankind, and Allah dislikes corruption" (2:205).

The Prophet said: "You are guardians, responsible for your wards".[33] He also said: "A Muslim must hear and obey whether he likes it or dislikes it, except when ordered to commit a sin, in which case there shall be no hearing nor obedience," adding "obedience is only in righteousness," as was stated by Abū Bakr.

Accordingly, a ruler can be removed if he acts in contravention of his official duties, or commits immoral, oppressive acts, or violates the commandments of the Qur'an and Sunnah.

CONCLUSION

It is clear, therefore, that Māwardī, being part of the Abbasid Administration (*qāḍī*) and envoy, analyzed in detail the late Abbasid political history. He summarized the opinion of all jurisconsults on the criteria for the selection of the Caliph, the qualities of the Caliph and Wise Elders, selection of the wazirs and governors, jihad for public good, judiciary, *ṣalāh*, imam, Hajj administration, zakah, *fay* and *ghanīmah*, *jizyah* and *kharāj*, regional statutes, revival of dead lands, reserve and common lands, grants and concessions, *dīwān*, criminal actions, and ombudsman or public order (*ḥisbah*).[34]

While giving an interpretation, such as the ruler may apply Shari‘ah, but may be unjust, he stopped short of passing judgment (ijtihad), being constrained by his office of judge. However, it was left to later scholars like Rashid Riḍa and Mawdudi, who were courageous enough to criticize the policy of ‘Uthmān for retaining Mu‘āwiyah for nearly 20 years as Governor, thus making him very popular. Also, most jurisconsults agree that in Islam there was no hereditary transfer of power. Another important principle is *Shūrā* by the ruler, which became extinct when the monarchy replaced the Guided Caliphate. In the early Umayyad period, a Caliph gave a long Friday Sermon till ‘*Aṣr* (afternoon prayer); on objection by a Companion to fear Allah, his head was chopped off. It was no wonder, therefore, that many righteous jurisconsults like Abū Ḥanīfah and Mālik refrained from accepting posts such as that of Chief Judge, suffering torture in prison as a result.[35]

Shūrā is mandatory both on the ruler and the ruled as ‘*ibādah,* and refraining from it is a sin for, "Allah's hand is on collectivity" as happened at Badr and ‘Uḥud, when Allah gave the Muslims victory.

There is no veto in Islam. When given, the *Shūrā* is binding on the ruler. Even the dispatch of an army to Syria by the first Caliph, Abū Bakr, following the Prophet's death, his fighting the apostates who refused to pay zakah, and the Ummah's denial of zakah money to early Muslims for *ta'līf al-qulūb* (winning over) on the grounds that Islam had gained strength, were the outcome of *Shūrā* (consultation).

Further, it is very clear that early jurists exercised ijtihad in their time, although their decision was not binding on later generations. Validation of ijtihad is dependent on *Maṣlaḥah* (public good), ‘*Urf, Istiḥsān, Qiyās* and is therefore a continuing exercise in the light of changing circumstances, as has been mentioned by Imam Mālik and the other three Ḥanafī imams. Even Madinah scholars differed from the Iraqi school, yet they did not accuse each other of unbelief, as was done in later periods, a practice prevalent now.[36]

On the basis of ‘*Urf',* Islam retained such practices as Hajj, the removal of idols, and a ban on naked circumambulation or *Ṭawāf* of the Ka‘bah. On the same analogy, present and future principles, concepts, and methodology in the Western political system can be adopted, provided they are compatible with the Shari‘ah, the Qur'an, and the Sunnah. If Islam is universal, and there is no doubt that it is, it has to allow room for the acceptance of what is good in the light of research and practices evolved in the modern world. That is what the International Institute of Islamic Thought (IIIT) is doing and its scope has also included political science from a *Tawḥīdī* (Islamic) perspective.

While accepting the possibility of errors, the writer could not cover such aspects of political theory as the sovereignty of Allah, the concept of *Ḥukūmāh Ilahiyyah*, theocracy versus democracy, and its compatibility with the Islamic political system. Likewise, the participation of Muslims in the polity of non-Muslim countries (*Dār al-Ḥarb* or *Dār al-Bayʿah*) has been omitted, being outside the purview of this chapter, even though Dr. Hamidullah[37] considers that in the Makkan period, the affairs of Muslims were not decided under the law of polytheists, but by the Prophet, amounting to a state within a state. This and other topics mentioned above require further research.[38]

4

Intellectual History of Euro-American Jurisprudence and the Islamic Alternative

PETER M. WRIGHT

ABSTRACT

The legal systems that presently prevail in Europe, the Americas, and in polities colonized and formerly colonized by Europe evolved in specific historical contexts and cultural milieus. Nevertheless, they share certain common presumptions that are rarely articulated or exposed to critical scrutiny. It is the task of this chapter to begin to articulate these common presumptions and to attempt to engage them constructively by a comparative study of a rival legal system, such as may be found in accepted principles of Islamic Shariʿah.

In the American context, the notion is widespread that research on a familiar subject [by virtue of the subject's very familiarity] ought to be easily accessible. But much Continental work in social science challenges this idea at a fundamental level. It asserts that the mysteries of social existence are densest, not in the behavior of far-off exotic peoples, but in our own everyday usages. Here, familiarity has bred an ignorance which arises not from the strangeness of the object of investigation, but from its very transparency. Living within it, so thoroughly suffused with its assumptions that it is even hard to recall just when we adopted them, we tend to lose the critical perspective which makes 'social science' more than simply a recital of what everyone already knows. The common sense of things, the knowledge everyone is sure to have, is precisely the starting point for the investigations of such a social science.[1]

EURO-AMERICAN JURISPRUDENCE   39

A MOST DIFFICULT intellectual task that we routinely face is to identify what is always before us; our familiarity with a thing is often precisely what conceals it from us. Sometimes it is even easier to consider first what something familiar is not, before we can begin to say adequately just what it is. This is the approach taken by the French thinker, Tzvetan Todorov, in a remarkable "essay in general anthropology," *Life In Common,* originally published in 1995 and then translated into English in 2001. I prefer to open these "preliminary remarks" with reference to Todorov's essay because I am about to attempt an explication of the familiar. I do not trust myself to give an adequate account of the obvious – or what seems to me *should* be obvious – without assistance.

Todorov's essay begins with a chapter entitled "A Brief Look at the History of Thought." Now this characterization offers an object lesson in the very problem that I have just identified and on account of which I have turned to Todorov for aid. Despite Todorov's inclusive title, the "history of thought," he does not mean the history of all thought, but the history of European and Euro-American thought exclusively. This assertion is obvious from Todorov's opening sentence ("As one studies the broad currents of European philosophical thought …"), although he omits any such qualification in his chapter heading.[2] A most difficult intellectual task that we routinely face is to identify what is always before us. Even the best among us fail to meet the challenge.

I am willing to forgive Todorov this initial blind spot because he manages to move beyond it and expose to view what I find to be a fascinating, if "invisible," familiar. He states that "As one studies the broad currents of European philosophical thought …" one discovers (although few seem to have noticed) that a "definition of man" – of the human being – begins to emerge. It is a definition that presents human beings as essentially "solitary" and "nonsocial" creatures. Todorov goes so far as to characterize all of the "broad currents of European philosophical thought" as "antisocial traditions." He then proceeds by way of example to offer evidence in support of this astonishingly sweeping assertion.[3]

Before we allow ourselves to be carried away with the tide of Todorov's argument, we must make a threshold observation. Even if we grant Todorov his characterization of "the broad currents of European philosophical thought" as essentially antisocial, philosophy is one thing, law another. Todorov, a literary critic by training, develops his thesis from readings of the relevant philosophical literature. However, what place does a book such as Todorov's rightfully occupy in a discussion of European and/or Euro-American legal systems?

None, I would suggest, unless a link can be established between the intellectual traditions that Todorov identifies and the social institutions that we wish to consider. To find such a link, it may prove helpful to move beyond Todorov's book – or perhaps behind it – and review the work of yet another French intellectual, Pierre Bourdieu.

Reading Bourdieu is never easy. He favors complex sentences composed of strings of subordinate clauses separated by commas. He has also developed a unique vocabulary – his own conceptual apparatus – though one that has not gained wide currency on this side of the Atlantic. Consequently, I introduce Bourdieu's work into this discussion at the risk of trying the reader's patience. I would not do so if I knew a better alternative.

Bourdieu turned his attention to European and Euro-American legal systems in an article which he published in volume 38 of *The Hastings Law Journal*. In this article, Bourdieu outlined what he called a "rigorous science of law," which he identified with his own enterprise as a social scientist, and distinguished this science from "what is normally called jurisprudence in that the former takes the latter as its object of study."[4]

From this vantage point, Bourdieu hopes to avoid entanglement in the debate about law that preoccupies European legal scholars: whether the law develops in "absolute autonomy … to the social world" (a position Bourdieu identifies as "Formalist") or whether law is merely a "reflection, or a tool in the service of dominant social groups" (a school of thought Bourdieu identifies as "Instrumentalist"). Bourdieu charts a third way that contains elements reminiscent of the other two, but which is not identical with either and which possesses unique properties of its own.[5]

In charting this third way, Bourdieu makes use of his own conceptual apparatus – most importantly, for our purposes, the notion of *habitus*. As summarized by the translator of this article, Richard Terdiman, *habitus* indicates "habitual, patterned ways of understanding, judging, and acting" which arise from one's "particular position" as a member of a given social structure. Terdiman writes: "The notion asserts that different conditions of existence – different educational backgrounds, social statuses, professions, and regions – all give rise to forms of habitus characterized by internal resemblance within the group ..."[6] This concept seems to me to owe much to the sociology of knowledge: one's understanding of the world is preconditioned and mediated by one's membership in society. As Bourdieu himself puts it:

> Shaped through legal studies and the practice of the legal profession on the basis of a kind of common familial experience, the prevalent dispositions of the legal habitus operate like categories of perception and judgment that structure the perception and judgment [of legal practitioners.]

> There is no doubt that the practice of those responsible for "producing" or applying the law owes a great deal to the similarities which link the holders of this quintessential form of symbolic power to the holders of worldly power in general, whether political or economic. This is so despite the jurisdictional conflicts which may set such holders of power in opposition to each other. The closeness of interests, and, above all, the parallelism of habitus, arising from similar family and educational backgrounds, fosters kindred world-views. Consequently, the choices which those in the legal realm must constantly make between differing or antagonistic interests, values, and world-views are unlikely to disadvantage the dominant forces. For the ethos of legal practitioners, which is at the origin of these choices, and the immanent logic of the legal texts, which are called upon to justify as well as to determine them, are strongly in harmony with the interests, values, and world-views of these dominant forces.[7]

Bourdieu places the "interests, values, and world-views" of those who hold and wield what he characterizes as "this quintessential form of symbolic power," the power to make and apply law, in an institutional context. Those who populate legal institutions share not only their membership in their common "field" (another word that occupies an important place in Bourdieu's conceptual apparatus), but also a common habitus, a way of being-in-the-world fostered by "similar family and educational backgrounds." It is here, I suggest, that one may entertain a link between Todorov's "broad currents of European philosophical thought" and the law. These intellectual traditions are not so much consciously appropriated by lawyers and judges as they are simply imbibed by them throughout the processes of socialization that precede their formal legal training. They do not typically take the form of well-wrought ideological positions but as inchoate assumptions, presumptions, and prejudices. They are the spectacles through which any decently educated and socialized individual in the West will view the world.

One need not be a French intellectual to appreciate the significance of the social phenomena Bourdieu describes. John Simmons's 1992 study of Locke's theory of rights opens with a series of observations that are consonant with the notion of habitus – without recourse to Bourdieu's social scientific jargon:

> Most people in the English-speaking world [and many outside it] have a practical, nonacademic acquaintance with the Lockean theory of rights. A commitment to [parts of] that theory grounds many of their social and political practices and institutions, and, as a result, guides many of their commonsense judgments about right and wrong, just and unjust. It provides prominent and comforting landmarks in their moral world. American school children learn by rote [or, at least, used to learn] some of the content of the Lockean theory: "that all men are created equal, that they are endowed by their Creator with certain inalienable rights, that among these are life, liberty, and the pursuit of happiness."[8]

I would hasten to add that they learn as well what Locke conceived to be the seat or location of the Divine endowment – the individual self or soul – with the concomitant belief that every individual self or soul has the prerogative to assert his or her rights as against every other individual and/or against society itself.

Todorov argues his thesis that the predominant intellectual traditions of the West are, at bottom, anti-social traditions, in two distinct ways. The first way consists of a review of the major proponents of these traditions. Here we find a roll call of the usual suspects: Hobbes, Kant, the French materialists-encyclopedists – in short, the names which we often associate with that period of history known to Europeans as their "Enlightenment" and the thoughts which we associate with those names. The second way in which Todorov chooses to argue this thesis is in contrast: he juxtaposes those currents of European thought which he has identified as predominant with an exception to those very currents taken, in the eighteenth century (as Europeans traditionally reckon time), by the Swiss philosopher, Jean-Jacques Rousseau. Todorov suggests that Rousseau's understanding of the human being is not only an exception to the rule of European and Euro-American thinking on the subject, but also represents "a real revolution" in thought. According to Todorov, Rousseau "became the first to formulate a new conception of man as a being who *needs others*."9 Without belaboring the point, I feel obliged again to expose the Eurocentrism in Todorov's statement of his case: Rousseau may well be the first European to formulate a new conception of man as a being who needs others, yet, as we shall see, Rousseau's European exception is an Islamic commonplace. In any event, the "assumptions" which Todorov characterized as latent in European philosophical thought are "antisocial" in the sense that they portray human beings as creatures who are so constituted that they do not need one another in Rousseau's sense of human necessity. And what sense is that? According to Todorov (and I concur with his reading), Rousseau insisted that "man brings to existence an innate insufficiency and that, therefore, each of us has a real need of others, a need to be *considered,* a 'need to attach his heart.'"10

Todorov asserts that the broad currents of European thought deny to human beings this "insufficiency." In European tradition, men and women are innately self-sufficient – particularly where the moral sense is concerned. European moral reflection has therefore focused upon the individual in isolation from others. According to Todorov, "The different versions of this asocial vision are easy to identify." Beginning with "the great moralists of the classical period", that is, the Stoics, "... [d]ealing with others is a burden to be discharged ..." – something one would do best to avoid, where possible. This tradition translated neatly into its successor, the Christianity of St. Augustine, whose *Confessions* exemplifies the intensely personal nature of the Augustinian encounter with God. In the waning days of the Medieval period, thinkers emerged who understood "[s]ociety and morality [to] conflict with human nature [by] ...impos[ing] rules of communal life on an essentially solitary being. It is this conception of man," writes Todorov, that "the concept (is) found in the most influential political and psychological theories of today."11 It is also, I would add, the unspoken anthropological presumption that pervades the European and Euro-American legal habitus. In the (North) American version, self-sufficiency is not merely a fact of being human; it is seen as a *desideratum,* a goal one should strive to realize in one's daily life. The implication is that, in order to be *fully* human, we must each learn to make our own way independent of the claims that others, our society, make upon us.

Rousseau's position, on the other hand, represents for Todorov the Great Road Not Taken: Western civilization's missed opportunity. Reading Todorov and Bourdieu together, we may begin to formulate an approach to the study of Euro-American legal institutions that reflects an appreciation for the following paradox: that the actors who populate and determine the tone and policy of these social institutions uncritically share certain anti-social presumptions.

This is Todorov's interpretation and it is one that I find compelling enough to take as a point of departure and examine, in its light, those legal institutions that have evolved under the aegis of European intellectual history. Such an undertaking is, admittedly, a monumental task; it is not one that I can hope to encompass in an essay which I have styled as "preliminary remarks." Be that as it may, I believe, as a scholar, I dare not avoid Malinowski's admonition that one "cannot study separately the institutions and mentality of a people. Only by investigating them side by side, by seeing how certain ideas correspond to certain social arrangements, can both aspects become intelligible."[12] Accordingly, I turn to yet another French intellectual, Michel Foucault, whose landmark study of Western penal institutions, *Discipline & Punish*, offers an original reading of the history of Western theory and practice of judicially authorized punishment.

Reading Foucault is no less challenging than reading Bourdieu. His analyses are sophisticated and nuanced. I do not pretend here to treat of Foucault's book with any critical depth. I wish only to suggest that Foucault's study of social institutions supports Todorov's thesis concerning European intellectual history in telling respects. Foucault situates Western penal institutions alongside other social institutions (for example, schools, hospitals etc.) as foci of social control. Each of these institutions individually and, increasingly, in concert with others, exercises subtle – and not so subtle – degrees of coercive influence over the individuals subject to its jurisdiction. Beneath the rhetoric of reform that often is invoked to characterize the evolution of the Western penal institution, Foucault finds a progressive movement toward more sophisticated forms of bureaucratic dominance over the human personality. For Foucault, the predominance of the prison over other forms of discipline and punishment in Western society must not be understood as a movement from barbarism to humanism; rather, it is a change – or, possibly, a refinement – of focus: from the exercise of coercion over human bodies to the exercise of coercion over the human soul.[13]

What Foucault intends by the word "soul" is not what that word has signified to Western ears over the course of Christendom's sway; neither is Foucault's intention completely incompatible with traditional understandings. For our purposes, it will suffice to take Foucault's use of the word "soul" as a marker for those aspects of human personality that have, heretofore, escaped bureaucratic interference: that small space left open to each one of us concerning which government has yet to express an interest – or found a means to subject to surveillance.

The prison's rise to predominance in Western societies represents for Foucault the latest effort on the part of the powerful in those societies to perfect the techniques of coercion and control that such groups have been honing since the advent of the Modern state:

> In several respects, the prison must be an exhaustive disciplinary apparatus: it must assume responsibility for all aspects of the individual, his physical training, his aptitude to work, his everyday conduct, his moral attitude, his state of mind; the prison, much more than the school, the workshop or the army, which always involved a certain specialization, is 'omni-disciplinary' ... Not only must the penalty be individual ... it must also be individualizing ... 'Alone in his cell, the convict is handed over to himself; in the silence of his passions and of the world that surrounds him, he descends into his conscience, he questions it and feels awakening within him the moral feeling that never entirely perishes in the heart of man' ... [T]his [is the] primary objective of carceral action: coercive individualization, by the termination of any relation that is not supervised by authority or arranged according to hierarchy.[14]

Foucault's prisons are "reformatories" in the sense that they are designed to impress permanently upon their inmates those asocial attributes which are expected of members of Western societies. When one leaves such a reformatory, one is expected to exemplify the socially acceptable antisocial attributes cultivated therein. The process of individualization that takes place in Foucault's prisons is one that attempts to reconcile individuals to a life of isolation from other individuals – for the sake, ostensibly, of their moral (and, therefore, civic) improvement. This process, by which individuals learn to accept their essential alienation from their neighbors, is one by which they are rendered sufficiently docile to be socially useful.[15]

The success of prisons as factories of individualization is demonstrated for Foucault by the fact that they are documented failures as factories of moral and/or civic improvement. "Detention," Foucault argues, "causes recidivism; those leaving prison have more chance than before of going back to it; convicts are, in a very high proportion, former inmates …"[16] The conclusions drawn by Foucault regarding Western penal institutions appears to be quite compatible with Todorov's reading of European intellectual history, *vis.*, that Rousseau was right about human beings needing one another. And if Rousseau was right, Western social institutions have congealed around an anthropology that is, at best, self-defeating. Or at least Western penal institutions have done so.

Although I would gladly linger with this tantalizing possibility, I think it may be more productive to move on to a discussion of a different set of "philosophical currents" that flow through a different model for juridical institutions. Let us put aside, for the moment, Europe and the West and consider the anthropology at the heart of Islamic Shariᶜah.

Before doing so, it is necessary to be clear from the outset what meaning Muslim scholars of Shariᶜah intend by that Arabic term. Perhaps it may be useful to begin with what they generally do *not* intend. As I read the literature, Shariᶜah does not have the meaning that most treatments in English assign to it, for example, "the body of Islamic sacred laws derived from the Qur'an, the Sunnah (q.v.) and the *aḥadīth* (q.v.)."[17] The laws themselves are the product of fiqh, or Islamic jurisprudence. Shariᶜah is something else – something more primitive, in a way, something that must be in place *before* the field of jurisprudence may be entered. Here, again, I find recourse to Bourdieu's conceptual apparatus most helpful. Because if Shariᶜah is ever to be distinguished from the legacy of misunderstanding that has accumulated around it in the West, we, in the West, will need to learn a new vocabulary; we will need to develop a conceptual apparatus that is capable of bearing the polysemous freight that native speakers of Arabic take for granted when they use their words. To develop an appropriate sense of the meaning of Shariᶜah, it is useful to think in terms of *habitus* – those "habitual, patterned ways of understanding, judging, and acting" which arise from one's "particular position" as a member of a given social structure.

With this meaning – or approximation of the meaning – of Shariʿah in hand, it is arguable that Shariʿah belongs to a distant – though by no means forgotten – past. Because Shariʿah does not reside in the body of laws developed over the centuries by Muslim jurists, one cannot simply return to those laws, or attempt to implement them, in the hope that, in the process, Shariʿah will be revived. The role of Shariʿah is to animate fiqh – not *vice versa*; it must therefore first reside in the Muslim jurists themselves – in their "habitual, patterned ways of understanding, judging, and acting" as these are determined by a given jurist's "particular position" as a member of an Islamic social structure.

The most interesting questions one can ask today about Islamic sacred law are these: what is the prevailing social structure in those places where Muslim jurists presently practice and how does it compare with the social structure that prevailed when the body of fiqh that those jurists have inherited was developed? These questions open the door to an even more momentous question of philosophical import: in what sense may one speak of Shariʿah as a present reality?

These are not questions to which I intend to essay an answer – at least not within the confines of the present chapter. Fortunately, I have smaller fish to fry. There is no question that Muslim jurists developed a body of sacred law over a period of several centuries, and that they did so within a particular *habitus*. A description of this habitus may afford us some insight into what Shariʿah once was – and we shall leave aside for the present those questions which would lead us to speculate what, if anything, Shariʿah now is or may some day prove to be.

Few scholars writing in English have offered any satisfactory account of the *habitus* from which emerged the great schools of thought responsible for the past production of Islamic sacred law. Karen Armstrong, however, is a recent exception that proves the rule. In the Preface to her *Islam: A Short History,* Armstrong offers a succinct description of a distinctively Islamic way of inhabiting space and time:

> In Islam, Muslims have looked for God in history. Their sacred scripture, the Qur'an, gave them a historical mission. Their chief duty was to create a just community in which all members, even the most weak and vulnerable, were treated with absolute respect. The experience of building such a society and living in it would give them intimations of the divine, because they would be living in accordance with God's will. A Muslim had to re-

deem history, and that meant that state affairs were not a distraction from spirituality but the stuff of religion itself. The political well-being of the Muslim community was a matter of supreme importance. Like any religious ideal, it was almost impossibly difficult to implement in the flawed and tragic conditions of history, but after each failure Muslims had to get up and begin again.[18]

One cannot help but recognize in this passage a counter-tradition to that which Todorov discovered in the "broad currents of European philosophical thought on the definition of what is human." Dealing with others is not a burden best avoided; in fact, the notion that it is even possible to engage in such avoidance is not within the purview of Islamic thought. One's duty to God demands that one *consider* the Other – and not merely as a given part of the landscape, as so much furniture – but also as an essential aspect of one's own moral, spiritual, civic, well-being. Isolation is not an option.

Armstrong bases her interpretation of the mission of Islam upon her study of the history of Islam and Muslims; however, the impetus of this mission originates in an anthropology contained in the Qur'an–indeed, in its very language. Although the Arabic root *Hamzah-Nūn-Sīn* appears throughout the Qur'an as a general term for humankind, it is also used to signify persons who seek after familiarity, intimacy. The implication of this etymological exercise (which, traditionally, occupies an honored place in Qur'anic exegesis) is that Islamic tradition includes the belief that human beings need one another – an anthropology not unlike that which Todorov attributes to Rousseau.

As with Western individualism, Islamic sociality presents juridical entailments: "The central notion of Justice in the Shariʿah is based on mutual respect of one human being by another," writes A. R. Doi:

> The just Society in Islam means the society that secures and maintains respect for persons through various social arrangements that are in the common interests of all members. A man as *Khalīfat-Allah* (viceregent [sic] of Allah) on earth must be treated as an end in himself and never merely as a means since he is the cream of Creation and hence the central theme of the Qur'an. What is required is the equal integrity of each person in the society and his loyalty to the country concerned which in turn will make it the duty of the society to provide equally for each person's pursuit of happiness.[19]

General statements of principle such as the foregoing abound in treatises written by Muslim scholars on the meaning of Shariʿah. To the Western ear, such pronouncements are likely to be dismissed as vague, platitudinous, or utopian fluff; yet Shariʿah, as habitus, is not reducible to a set of rules – much less to what common law lawyers like myself refer to, in our own legal tradition, as "black letter law." Notice Doi's reference to "social arrangements," as opposed to, say, the "legal system" or "penal institutions." This is not a question of idiosyncratic word choice. Islamic sacred law is predicated not upon the establishment of certain juridical institutions, but rather, upon the creation of a certain kind of community. Such a community, according to Doi, is socially egalitarian: "The treatment accorded by the Shariʿah made the aristocracies of birth, race, wealth, language, the features which vary from person to person, all suspect as disrespectful of persons." Such a community is also economically equitable:

> The Shariʿah, it should be noted, gives priority to human welfare over human liberty. Muslims as well as non-Muslims living in a Muslim state are duty bound not to exploit common resources to their own advantage, destroy good producing land, and ruin the potential harvest or encroach upon a neighbor's land. Since a man in Islam is not merely an economic animal, each person's equal right to life, to a decent level of living, has priority over the so called economic liberty.[20]

It bears remarking that such issues are the subject of continuing legislation and litigation in modern Western societies; Doi's point is that Shariʿah assumes the resolution of such issues – or, at the very least, that the resolution of such issues should not be left to the pendulum swings of party politics or judicial gerrymandering. He asserts:

> Behind every legal, social or political institution of Islam, there is a divine sanction which every believer is expected to reverence no matter where he lives. He cannot change his own whims into laws. There are the limits of Allah [Ḥudūd-Allah] which are imposed in order to curtail man's ambitions and devices.

The limits of Allah, Doi continues, are the two poles of "ḥalāl" (permissible) and "ḥarām" (prohibited) that are contained in the Qur'anic Revelation and are elaborated by Prophetic pronouncement and example in the hadith literature. These poles set the boundaries within which the Islamic community is free to define itself as a polity with distinctive faith and moral commitments.[21]

To this point, I have made no mention of specific juridical institutions contemplated by Shariʿah or instantiated in the history of Islamic societies. This is because, in the former case, it is difficult to say what specific juridical institutions, if any, *are* contemplated by Shariʿah; and the latter case is itself rendered problematic by the difficulties raised in the former. I do not wish to deny the rich history of fiqh (attempts to apply Shariʿah), its elaboration by the ʿalims (the learned) and *Fuqahā'* (those who are particularly learned in matters of fiqh), or even the reality of decisions rendered in particular cases by, say, a village *qāḍī* (judge). I wish only to affirm Armstrong's observation regarding the Muslim commitment to the creation of a just community (as expressed in the broad outlines of Shariʿah): "Like any religious ideal, it was almost impossibly difficult to implement in the flawed and tragic conditions of history…" Consequently, the extent to which any particular juridical decision conforms to the requirements of Shariʿah is always a matter of debate among Muslims – because the ideal rarely finds adequate expression in the messy circumstances of daily life.

This is not to suggest that societies with majority Muslim populations have failed, throughout the world and history, to create viable juridical institutions. However, majority Muslim societies function with a set of juridical instincts that are distinguishable from those that prevail in the non-Muslim West. One evidence of this difference may be inferred from the types of sanctions traditionally made available to the Muslim community under Shariʿah, compared with those utilized in Western societies. If we accept the verdict of Foucault, Western individualism finds juridical expression in the prison system. Individualism is privileged at the expense of the community – as expressed by the familiar adage that it is sometimes necessary "to destroy the village in order to save it." Muslim communitarianism, whether in its ideal (Shariʿah) or applied (fiqh) expression, is unwilling to take such a risk. As a result, incarceration – though not unknown under Shariʿah-based systems – has never been regarded by majority Muslim societies as a great civilizing or humanizing advance over other forms of sanction.

Be that as it may, I would be remiss if I failed to acknowledge what I take to be a corollary anthropological intuition common to Muslims: an intuition that the form of understanding which Bourdieu termed *habitus* is embodied, if at all, in individuals and not – for lack of a better term – corporations. Islamic emphasis upon the collective never rules out the indispensable role of the individual in creating the just community.[22]

Such considerations suggest a paradox that appears to me to afflict both Muslim communitarianism and Western individualism – a paradox recently articulated by the American philosopher Richard Eldridge in an insightful study of Wittgenstein's later work. Eldridge asks: Which is to be changed first, human character or sociopolitical institutions? Change in human character and change in sociopolitical institutions presuppose one another with no evident way to break into this circle of presuppositions. One will fail in trying directly to educate and elevate the human beings who are formed under sociopolitical institutions, and one will fail in trying directly to change the sociopolitical institutions that express human character. "All improvement in the political sphere is to proceed from the ennobling of character – but how under the influence of a barbarous constitution is character ever to become ennobled?"[23]

As a general proposition, I would suggest that thoughtful Muslims and non-Muslims could be expected to agree as to the validity of this conundrum. Where the two would potentially part company is in the response to the problem. In so far as the Muslim understands his/her role in history as one of refashioning sociopolitical institutions in conformity with Shariʿah – as the Divinely ordained "way to break into this circle of presuppositions" – one could expect sociopolitical activism. The response of non-Muslims in the West would be, predictably, more varied, more individualized. It could be anticipated to run the gamut from sociopolitical activism (such as we find today with the so-called "Christian right") to resigned quietism. This is not to suggest, however, that the latter course is not open to Muslims. L. C. Brown has recently argued that political quietism has a long and distinguished career among Muslims living in majority Muslim polities.[24] Shariʿah may be argued to authorize the same varied and individualized responses among Muslims that one would anticipate finding among non-Muslims in the West, given the appropriate circumstances. The essentializing tendencies of a legal scholar such as Doi – or of an historian such as Armstrong, or our French intellectuals – should spur the reader on to more thorough investigation and greater efforts to articulate the sociopolitical and historical contexts, inculcating the *habitus*, by and through which laws are promulgated, interpreted, applied, and enforced.

5

Middle Eastern Origins of Modern Sciences

DILNAWAZ A. SIDDIQUI

A S THE SAYING GOES, there is nothing new under the sun. Since time immemorial, human beings have inherited existing knowledge from previous generations, improved upon it by adapting it to their present needs, and transmitted it to future generations. Besides this vertical transmission, the transfer of knowledge also occurs horizontally from one place or culture to another by the continual exchange of ideas. Human civilization has been built over a period of about seven millennia with its beginnings along the banks of Shatt al-Arab, the Nile, and the Indus. Knowledge has been gathered through patient observation, experience, as well as serendipity. Prior to the Greco-Roman civilization, scholars of Khalidiah, Babylon, Phoenicia, Egypt, India, and China had greatly contributed to human understanding of the universe up to the seventh century BC. Greek learning progressed up to the second century BC, when it succumbed to the iron fist of Rome. The latter failed to encourage creativity, innovation and scientific investigation. During this time, Greek contributions lapsed into oblivion until they were discovered and improved upon for onward transmission by Muslims.

The responsibility of coordinating such exchanges falls, by default or by design, upon the contemporary dominant power(s). Since the sixteenth century, the West has greatly expanded its inheritance by coordinating, improving, and disseminating its knowledge. Its contribution to modern science and technology has remained unmatched and is likely to remain so for quite some time to come. Especially revolutionary and mind-boggling has been the digitization of data, images, and sound, as well as the miniaturization of tools such as wireless computer technology supported by space-based global positioning systems.

Unlike in other cultures, the social science tradition as developed in Europe has played down the similarities among various cultures and civilizations and exaggerated the dissimilarities for its own politico-economic reasons. One major reason for this practice was to conceal the contributions of the colonized nations to human civilization. Such a tendency helped perpetuate the notion of "the white man's burden to civilize the world" and thus exploit with impunity their natural and technological resources.

THE RATIONALE

One might ask why we should discuss the heyday of a nation left so far behind others in the march of scientific and technological progress. What good is it to keep harping on about our past laurels in the spirit of Pidaram sultan bood [My father was king]! without going into the causes for our miserable plight today? The answer is that there is more than one single reason for invoking our past.

The modern world is now experiencing three major trends: (1) revolution in the area of information technologies; (2) globalization; and (3) privatization. It is the first, especially the digitization of information, that has brought various peoples closer together to interact with one another in the global trade arena, and has allowed individuals access to information and knowledge (if not wisdom) in an unprecedented manner. Thus, these trends have made nations more interdependent. The increased interdependence is both enriching and troubling in that it can provoke a scramble for limited global resources and commodities and in turn generate conflicts never faced earlier. To counter potential conflicts, we need to remove the cultural stereotypes promoted by colonialists as a policy to "divide, conquer, and rule." Realistic mutual understanding by a dialog of civilizations rather than a clash of civilizations is a must for global peace with justice to prevail. Besides this moral imperative, it is also incumbent on the part of the academe to amend the historical records about the origins of Western higher education and scientific development.

For us in the West, it is also vital to cope with increased competition in global trade. The neo-colonialist desire of Darwinian domination needs to be civilized through fair competition and healthy cooperation. For sustained development our media also needs to cultivate in the audience a taste for truth and wisdom, for objective rational and responsible journalism instead of resorting to sex, violence, and sensationalism based on the "If it bleeds, it leads" type of programming. Pompous pride and complacency need to be replaced with an accurate understanding of our own strengths and weaknesses. A valid assessment of their past accomplishments and present predicament can enable Muslims to educate themselves and their future generations properly, and, in turn, enable them to plan realistically their further progress with great confidence.

Moreover, Muslims should also compensate for their own failure to tell the world their own story, which has been distorted by ignorance, arrogance, and often by malfeasance of anti-Islamic forces of material greed and bigotry. Without being defensive, Muslims ought to fill this knowledge gap in cross-cultural understanding.

CONTRIBUTIONS TO SCIENCE IN GENERAL

One of the attributes of science is that it is incremental and cumulative in nature. All scientifically and technologically developed nations have to pass through three phases: translation, coordination, and contribution.[1] They correspond to the three terms mentioned earlier: inheritance, improvement by innovation and creation, and transmission of knowledge. The intervals between these stages of development have varied according to the size of the existing knowledge base as well as the level of communication technology and speed of life as a whole. Thus, comparatively speaking, the narrower the inheritable knowledge base available to a generation, the more significant its contribution. The real value of the Muslim contribution to science ought to be assessed in view of the attitudinal change humanity experienced as a result of the advent of the Qur'an in the early sixth century AC.

James Burke, III, in his book *The Day the Universe Changed*,[2] asserts that prior to the advent of the Qur'an, human attitude toward nature was either that of fear or adoration and devotion. Created things that generated in humans a feeling of fear, like snakes and other dangerous animals, were worshipped to avert potential harm from them. Also venerated were beneficial elements of nature like water and fire, as well as animals, such as the cow etc. This veneration stemmed from humankind's gratitude for and admiration of their benefits.

The Qur'an, on the other hand, commanded human beings not to worship nature or any other part of Divine creation, but to bow down to their Creator, God. It invited human reason to search for His signs in creation and to draw lessons for their own evaluation and development. It is this pioneering role of Muslims on the basis of which their contribution ought to be compared with others. It was this revolutionary change in human attitude toward nature and the emphasis on reason that empowered Muslims to study nature from a scientific perspective, and to change the Universe forever, as it were. Again, it was the need of Muslims to fulfill their Islamic obligations that soon led them to develop mathematical formulae to calculate the passages and phases of the moon, and the location of the sun and various stars. The Qur'anic commandments concerning Zakah (welfare tax) and the shares of inheritors in the property bequeathed by parents and other relatives led to the development of calculus, trigonometry, and other devices for meticulous calculations.

Ibn al-Haytham's scientific method, erroneously attributed to Francis Bacon, led to phenomenal breakthroughs in different descriptions of natural sciences, which eventually led Europe toward its scholastic tradition and subsequently to the Renaissance.

By dint of the Qur'anic emphasis on the use of reason in all deliberations, Muslim scientists utilized a logico-empirical methodology of research and showed that there was no incompatibility between reason and Revelation. So unlike the Western tradition, from the Muslim scientists' perspective there has not been any conflict between science and religion. Alvi & Douglass[3] have identified five major reasons for the seminal development of Islamic science: (1) the immense esteem that Islam accords to scholarship; (2) the generous support by rulers and other affluent people that is available to scholars; (3) the willingness of Muslims to exchange ideas with others); (4) the Arabic language soon becoming a means of exchange of ideas throughout the Muslim world; and (5) the requirements of precision and punctuality in fulfilling Islamic duties. These notions are also affirmed by Colish.[4]

Historically, the knowledge of logic and geometry traveled from their Phoenician roots, originally from Iraq, to Egypt, and from Egypt to Greece. Muslim scholars then inherited them from the Greeks. They took astronomy and arithmetic from their Indo-Iranian origins and advanced them further to unprecedented levels.[5] Thus the entry of Muslims into the domain of organized knowledge helped humans to journey from "sa-pience" to "science".[6] On the subject of Islamic astronomy, Owen Gin-gerich[7] says that while astronomy withered in medieval Europe, it flouri-shed in Islam. Renaissance astronomers learned from the texts of Islamic scholars who had preserved and transformed the science of the ancient Greeks.

As has been pointed out earlier, Ibn al-Haytham's logico-empirical method enabled subsequent scientists to make phenomenal advances in numerous scientific disciplines, both basic and applied. Muslim scientists realized that the proper place for empiricism was only in the domain of physical phenomena, not in the metaphysical ones. However, once the latter were revealed, they made logical and rational sense evidenced by analysis of historical events. They, therefore, classified knowledge into two broad categories: revealed and acquired.

DEMOCRATIZATION OF KNOWLEDGE

The true significance of Islamic sciences can be understood only in the light of the Qur'anic concept of *Tawḥīd* (Unity), which encompasses all apparent diversity and interdependence. The interconnectedness of everything in the universe indicates the unity of cosmos. It logically follows that the creator or programmer of this supra-system must be One, otherwise there would be chaos instead of cosmos. The third unity is that of all forms of life. God clearly stated in the Qur'an: "We have created every living thing from water" (21:30, 24:45, 25:54). This revelation was made at a time when this "unity of life" was not part of human knowledge, indicating the divine origin of the Holy Qur'an. From the point of view of human relations, it is vital to appreciate the value of the fourth unity, namely, that of the human race, created from one single soul a pair, and from them the whole of humanity (2: 213, 4:1, 39:6, 31:28). This concept of "monogenesis" enabled Muslims to democratize all kno-wledge. A Sudanese scholar, Dr. A. Waheed Yousif,[8] who is currently an advisor to UNESCO, showed with documentary evidence that the twentieth-century 20-point lifelong education mission attributed to the United Nations, existed in practice during the early Muslim Abbasid period of the ninth century. There, for the first time in human history, access to all knowledge was made available to all, regardless of gender, race, ethnic origin, caste, class, nationality, or any other factor on which human beings have no control. Contrast this Islamic democratization of science and other forms of knowledge with the strict restrictions imposed by the privileged upon the downtrodden communities of all other cultures, including Greek, Roman, Persian, as well as Indian until recently.

During the seven hundred years of their leadership in science and technology (from the eighth to the fifteenth century), Muslims introduced these disciplines into higher education institutions, which they established throughout the regions ruled by them. Their universities in the Near East, North Africa, and Spain provided an open-access model for the Spanish Muslim universities at Toledo, Córdoba, and Seville attracting students also from other parts of Europe. They saw for themselves this democratization of learning and participative decision-making ("*Shūrā*") in the Muslim world. Once back in their own lands, they started to demand similar human rights from their Church and state. When they were denied these rights, they "protested" against the authorities, the Church and their feudal lords. This was precisely the origin of the Protestant movement in Europe.

The fifth unity in Islam is the unity of knowledge (truth). Unaware of the Qur'anic origin of this concept, the Harvard University Biologist, Edward Wilson,[9] presented the notion of "consilience" in his book of the same name, and stressed the need for interdisciplinary studies to overcome the myopic and disjointed pursuit of knowledge called "reductionism." From an Islamic perspective, this unity of knowledge and truth is nothing new.

The Muslim introduction of higher education, meticulous documentation, chapter making, Arabic numerals as well as other advanced applications of scientific knowledge to agriculture, medicine, architecture, and navigation led to the gradual advancement of Europe, eventually culminating into the Renaissance and Reform movements of the fifteenth and sixteenth centuries. The subsequent European colonization of the Americas resulted in the transfer of gold and other forms of wealth to Europe. During Muslim rule itself, centers of higher learning, research, and development, institutes, libraries, teaching hospitals, science laboratories and observatories became common in Muslim cities like Madinah, Damascus, Baghdad, Neshapore, Cairo, Qairawan, Córdoba, Toledo, and Seville.[10] This spree of institution building and development was emulated in Italy, France, Germany, England, and other parts of Europe.

Without Arabic numerals, advanced mathematical calculations could not be imagined given the limitation of Roman numerals. One can get a general idea of the scholarly activities of the Muslim world from Ibn al-Nadīm's *al-Fehrist* (tenth century),[11] which lists about four thousand prominent scientists and other scholars. Ibn Khallikan's biographical dictionary titled *Wafiyat al-ʿAʿyān wa Anbā' Abnā' al-Zamān* in seven volumes documents similar protagonists and their contributions in various fields of higher learning.[12] Many other reference resources have documented the Islamic cultural milieus and their history of various disciplines and sub-disciplines. Although numerous works of the Muslim scholars of that period have been translated from Arabic into modern European languages, it is estimated that about seventy thousand of them still remain untranslated.

CONTRIBUTIONS TO MATHEMATICS

As has been pointed out the Qur'anic commandments concerning the five daily prayers, the beginning and end of the fasting month of Ramadan, the distribution of inheritance, and the calculations of Zakah (welfare tax) called upon Muslims to be proficient in mathematics. Since an advanced language can be a means of communication in the humanities and social sciences, mathematics is considered to be the language of the natural and physical sciences. From the eighth century AC, Arabic became a language of higher learning, and mathematics written in Arabic numerals and symbols was the language of science for about seven centuries.

The Muslims introduced the Arabic numerals (originally borrowed from India), the concept of the zero, the decimal base of ten, and advanced mathematics into Europe. Prior to the eighth century, one had to write the letter "M" a thousand times to indicate one million. Imagine the ease of writing the same thing in only seven digits. By the ninth century, al-Khawārizmī had already given the world advanced algorithms or formulae. Notice that the English word algorithm is simply the Europeanized form of this Muslim name, al-Khawārizmī, who gave the world the first mathematical formula and trigonometry (sine, cosine, tangent, and co-tangent). The arithmetical and geometrical concepts and calculations of pi, hyperbole, series, and progressions, are also Muslim contributions to advanced mathematics that were later introduced into Europe.

It was the Muslim scholar, al-Mutawakkil al-Farghānī, who invented

Nilometer devices. More sophisticated devices like compasses were originally designed for determining the direction of the Kaʿbah, the cube-like Mosque of Prophet Abraham in Makkah, toward which all Muslims face while praying. Speaking of the inherent relationships between Islamic beliefs and values, Jane Norman states:

> Appreciation for a basic relationship between art and the religion of Islam increases with familiarity … Geometric motifs were popular with Islamic artists and designers in all parts of the world, at all times, and for decorating every surface … As Islam spread from nation to nation and region to region, Islamic artists combined their penchant for geometry with pre-existing traditions, creating a new and distinctive Islamic art. This art expressed the logic and order inherent in the Islamic vision of the universe.[13]

CONTRIBUTIONS TO CHEMISTRY

Their victory in Western China in the eighth century enabled the Muslims to benefit from contemporary Chinese technologies, such as paper-making, which they in turn introduced into the entire Muslim world including Spain. From there it was taken to the rest of Europe. This indeed was a revolutionary discovery leading to the wider dissemination of knowledge and democratization of learning. With the expansion in the exchange of ideas in the form of conveniently transportable books, and owing to the monogenetic concept of the equality of humankind, the earliest explosion of knowledge became possible throughout the world.

Muslims made tremendous progress in the field of chemistry, of which the Arabic *al-kīmiyah* is the etymological origin. They invented all the fundamental processes of chemical research and development, including sublimation, crystallization, evaporation, distillation, purification, amalgamation, and acidation (sulphuric, nitric, hydrochloric, and acetic). They then applied these processes to the manufacture of sugar, various types of dyes, alcohol, and arsenic for mostly medicinal purposes. By 950 AC, they had discovered how to heat mercury (Hg) to form mercuric oxide (HgO), noting that this chemical alteration does not cause any loss of weight of the basic substance itself. Muslims, owing to the Islamic emphasis on cleanliness and aesthetics, were fascinated by the chemical purification of gold to be used in making jewelry and preparing food, as well as in architectural decorations.

CONTRIBUTIONS TO PHYSICS AND ASTRONOMY

By the ninth century, Muslim scientists had discovered the laws of the strength of materials, mechanics, and stability. In his study of the laws of physics, al-Kindī scientifically described the phenomena of reflection and refraction of light, theories of sound and vacuum. The tenth and eleventh centuries saw the Muslim scientific principles related to the pendulum long before Galileo (1564–1642). Not until 1992 did the Pope forgive Galileo for the heresy of teaching that the Earth revolved around the Sun. In the 10th century, Ibn al-Haytham described and utilized his scientific method. It is worth noting that the term "science" was never used in Europe until 1340 AC, and it was only in 1840 AC that the word "scientist" was used in the English language for the first time. Ibn al-Haytham's findings on geometrical optics in 965 AC, which were later utilized in European inventions like cameras and sophisticated eyeglasses, are erroneously attributed to Snell (eighteenth and nineteenth centuries) as Snell's laws.

Muslim scientists also discovered the principles of homogeneity and heterogeneity in the context of rarefied air. Concepts and kinds of aberrations of images were explored and utilized in manufacturing lenses and mirrors. Not only did they know that light has velocity but they also compared velocities of light and sound and found that the former was greater than the latter. They studied and formulated laws of mechanics and hydrostatics, which they used in determining tensions of various types of surfaces, specific gravity and density of different forms of matter.

The concept of earth's gravity was known to Abū al-Fatḥ ʿAbd al-Raḥmān al-Khāzinī in the twelfth century, that is, several centuries before Isaac Newton, who only further refined it. It was al-Khāzinī himself who also explained the natural phenomenon of the rainbow in optical terms. He is credited with designing many astronomical instruments described in his *Mīzān al-Ḥikmah*.[14]

ʿUmar al-Khayyām of the twelfth century, who is known to the Western world only as a poet of the Persian *rubāʿiyyāt* (quatrains), made remarkable contributions to mathematics as well. He refined calendar calculations, by pointing to the existence of a one-day error in 5,000 years instead of the 3,330 years presumed earlier. Another Muslim, Ulugh Beg of Samarqand, further refined his calculations. Al-Khawārizmī, who has been mentioned above for his contributions to mathematics, was also the founding father of Islamic astronomy. Several centuries before Galileo, he and his followers had known the earth to be spherical, and he himself had calculated distances between various cosmic bodies.

The ninth-century scientist and astronomer, Abū Maʿashar, had accurately drawn latitudes and longitudes, discovered the relationship between the phases of the Moon and the ocean tides, scientifically explained lunar and solar eclipses, and refined calculations of the differential in the earth's circumference at different points of the globe. It was he who very accurately measured and explained the length of the terrestrial degree to be 56.67 Arabic miles.

Al-Saʿati Khurasānī, who is named after his invention of the clock (sāʿah: also time), of the twelfth century built a clock tower in Damascus, Syria. It was the Muslim geographer, al-Idrīsī, who presented King Roger II with the gift of his silver globe. Abdur Rahim identified and named about a thousand stars, and explained the elliptical paths of cosmic bodies in the known solar system. He is also credited with his significant researches in other fields like agriculture, architecture, literature, and linguistics.

In the field of applied physics, al-Jazzarī in the thirteenth century proved his prominence in his book dealing with the subject of hydraulic appliances, *Kitāb al-Maʿrifah wa al-Hiyal al-Handasah*. His contemporary, Najm al-Rammah, gained fame in his exhaustive volume on pyrotechnic techniques and devices, for both defense and ceremonial uses.

In 845 AC, that is hundreds of years before Darwin, al-Naẓẓām presented the theory of evolution. Within the same time frame, al-Jāḥiẓ wrote a voluminous treatise on animals, their struggle for survival and adaptation to physical environments. As early as the ninth century, al-Ḥāsib wrote a volume on the benefits of precious stones. Later, in the thirteenth century, his co-professional, al-Tifāshī, improved his work and added his studies on 24 precious stones and their affective and medicinal properties. Many others like al-Jawāliqī, ʿAbd al-Mumin, and al-Dhāmirī, made immense contributions to knowledge with their treatises on zoology and anatomy, especially on horses and their breeding.

Al-Dimashqī made his mark in botanical studies on plant pathologies, categorizing plants as living beings with a distinctive gender. Al-Bayrūnī, generally renowned as a historian, discovered the origin or source of the Indus Valley and its civilization. He also observed that the number of petals in flowers vary between 3 and 6, or they are 8. They never number 7 or 9. These and many other Muslim scientists left a rich scholarly legacy in Africa, Asia, and Europe.

DECLINE OF MUSLIM SCIENCES

The question is often raised of why Muslims at some point in history stopped developing in the fields of science and technology. There were many factors, both internal and external, affecting their stagnation and decline. Historically, in the case of most dominant powers, arrogance, ignorance of other societies and their state of development, and topsy-turvy priorities have been the major causes of internal weaknesses. Successes and their sustenance call for a balanced approach to different demands of human life, of body, mind, and soul. When this moderation is disturbed anomie sets in.

In its heyday, Islam was practiced as a comprehensive way of life. An overemphasis on its spiritual aspect continued to reduce its original scope. Consequently, many crucial concepts associated with it also diminished. The concept ʿIbādah (worship), which originally meant any practical act pleasing to God, became mere ritualistic prayers. The nawāfil any extra deeds of charity, turned into only excessive ritual prayers; and the concept of seeking knowledge became confined to mere theological learning. The roles of reason and creativity were played down even in areas where they were originally permissible, such as in the economic, political, and social domains.

The Muslims perhaps ignored the illustrative dialog between the Prophet and his Companion, Maʿādh ibn Jabal, when the latter was being dispatched to the governorship of Yemen. On this occasion, Maʿādh, in response to the Prophet's question of how he would rule there, had said that in cases where there was no clear-cut answer in the Qur'an and the Sunnah (Prophet's Sayings), he would do ijtihad. That is, he would form his own rational judgment from a pragmatist and problem-solving perspective. The answer had obviously satisfied and pleased the Prophet.

Moreover, there had been an internal debate and later a showdown between the Muʿtazilites, who were influenced by the Hellenistic starkly rationalistic analysis, and the Ashaʿarites, who had the theological approach to even new issues facing the the Ummah (the global Muslim community). The latter were traditionalists who relied on the analogical interpretations to the extent that they assumed that early scholars of Islam had finally interpreted the Qur'an and Sunnah for all times and climes. This myopic mindset of the traditionalists was not without reason. They had seen the excesses of Hellenistic hypocrisy in ignoring the limits of human reason in the form of fallacious acceptance of over-relativism, which is bedeviling contemporary thinking in almost all walks of life. While some rulers took advantage of the misuse of creativity and innovation in the name of ijtihad, others sided with the traditionalists in suppressing even the genuine use of all rational tools of development.

The sad result of this conflict between *riwāyah* (tradition) and *dirāyah* (rationalism) was the stagnancy and closure of the doors of rational and analytical genius of Muslim scholars and scientists. The religious scholarship became restricted to memorization of quotations and copying of old manuscripts from past scholars. The lone major voices since the eighteenth century urging the revival of ijtihad included Ibn Wahhāb, Shāh Waliullāh, Sir Syed Ahmed Khan, Jamaluddin Afghani, and Mohammed Abdu, as well as Mohammed Iqbal and Mawdudi. All of them stressed the need for a balance between the blind adherence to traditions on the one hand and, on the other, bold yet cautious interpretation of the same traditions within the framework of the seminal sources of Islam, and in light of the context and demands of specific times and places. They urged the Ummah to distinguish between *ijtihad-e-muṭlaq* (absolute exertion) through scholarly consensus and *ijtihad-e-idhāfī* (relative exertion) by renewing the old principles of Shariᶜah to handle new situations facing the community.

With regard to external challenges, the Muslim community has faced historical events such as the eleventh-century Crusades, the siege of Baghdad by the Mongols in 1258, expulsion from Spain in 1492, the end of the Caliphate in 1922, communism and colonialism, and more recently neo-colonialism resulting from oil politics accompanied by a powerful media onslaught, stereotyping victims as oppressors and oppressors as victims.

Other significant Muslim contributions are summarized below in Appendix 1 to this chapter. In view of Basheer Ahmed's chapter, in this book, on Muslim contributions to medicine as well as the chapters by other participants on social sciences and humanities, I have limited myself to works on the modern natural sciences only.[15]

APPENDIX ONE

Contributors to the Origins of World Science

PERIOD	SCIENTIST	REMARKS
721–815	Jābbir ibn Ḥayyān (Geber?) Founder of modern chemistry Logician Philosopher	3000 treatises on (Wālid ib Mālik)
		Scientific method concept and measurement of chemical balances
		Physics: mechanics
		Medicine: clinical pathology
		Contributed to the establishment of the first medical college at Damascus
Abbasid		*Bayt al-Ḥikmah* at Baghdad, Iraq
801–873	Abū Yūsuf al-Kindī (Al-Kindus) The Philosopher-Scientist of the Arabs	Precursor to al-Fārābī
		Description of the inhabited parts of the Earth
		Al-Shammāsiyyah Observatory, Baghdad
		Global postal service Book of Countries
		Contemporary of Hishām al-Kalbī and al-Yaʿqūbī
810–877	Ḥunayn ibn Isḥāq (Juannitius)	Physician-Philosopher
		Commentator on Galen

PERIOD	SCIENTIST	REMARKS
826–901	Thābit ibn Qurrah	3000 Volume of paraboloid 3rd degree figures in Geometry
		Mathematics Physics, Medicine, Astronomy
		Theory of Repidation
		Naval developments (Indian Ocean; Volga & Caspian Sea)
		Early maps
		Contemporaries: Balakhī, Maqdisī
?–863 (period of al-Maʿmūn)	M. al-Khawārizmi (algorith)	*Al-Jabr wa al-Muqābalah* (advanced algebra)
		Introduction of Arabic numerals into Europe
		Trinomial equations
		Astronomical tables
		Innovative computations
		Geography: shape of the Earth
		Observatory at al-Shammāsiyyah (with Naubakht)
865–925	Muḥammad al-Rāzī (Rhazes) (184 workers)	Smallpox/measles
		Observatory at Raqqa (Shiraz)
	Clinical Physician (Al-Ḥāwī): Continens anti-Aristotelian speculations	Contemporaries: Abū al-Wafā al-Buzjānī (4th degree equations), al-Karakhī

PERIOD	SCIENTIST	REMARKS
	Emphasis on time, space & causality in physics: direct observation of hard data	
	Music to alchemy Student of al-Ṭabarī	
870–950	Abū Naṣr al-Fārābī (Alpharabius)	Commentaries on works of Aristotle
	Philosopher	First classification of sciences
	Social Scientist	*Ikhwān al-Ṣafā Risālat al-Jamia*
?–956	Abūl Ḥasan al-Masʿūdī	Travelogues Meadows of Gold & Mines of
	Scientist Historian Anthropologist Geographer Geologist	Gems
980–1037	Abū ʿAlī ibn Sīna (Avicenna)	Shaykh al-Rais
	Medical scientist Physician	Cannon (*al-Qānūn*)
		Kitāb al-Shifāʾ
		Dār al-ʿIlm (Cairo) Observatory at Hamadan
		Scholarly conferences & proceedings
965–1039	Abū ʿAlī al-Haytham (Alhazen)	*Kitāb al-Mākir* (Optics) first eyeglasses (lathe)
	Mathematician Physicist (astro) Medical scientist Ophthalmologist	Scientific method Measurement of the Nile floods

PERIOD	SCIENTIST	REMARKS
		Observatory at Seville (Falah)
		Spherical and parabolic mirrors; refraction angles and velocity
		Principle of least time
		Contemporaries: Nusairī Khusro (Diary); al-Bakrī (Dictionary of Geography)
937–1051	Abū Rayḥān al-Bayrūnī	Commentaries on Aristotle
	Contributions to Mathematics; Astrophysics; Geography/Geodesy History and anthropology	Chronology of ancient nations
		Canon of al-Masʿūdī
		Astrolabes (used in navigation)
		Motions of the earth
		Levity and gravity of planets
		Elliptical orbits
		Contemporaries: al-Khāzinī (Physics): inclination impetus, momentum
?–1007	Abū al-Qāsim al-Majritī (Madrid, Córdoba)	Epistles of al-Ikhwān
		Observatory at Toledo (Zarqali)
	Mathematics, Chemistry, and Astronomy	
1058–1111	Abū Ḥāmid M. al-Ghazālī (Algazel)	The revival of religious sciences
		Contemporaries: Manṣurī/Nurī (Hospitals)
	Philosopher	Al-Idrīsī (Geography: the globe, and botany)
	Religious scientist	

PERIOD	SCIENTIST	REMARKS
12th c.	Raḥmān al-Khāzinī	Scientia vs. sapientia
	(The Greek)	Mechanics and hydrostatics
		Centers of gravity & balance of matter & balance of wisdom
		Standards: weights
1040–1130	Abū al-Fatḥ ʿUmar Khayyamī (Omar Khayyam)	Algebra
	Mathematician Scientist Poet	Quatrains (translated into English by Fitzgerald)
1126–1198	Abū al-Wāḥid M. ibn Rushd (Averroes of Córdoba)	Pure Aristotelian (38 commentaries)
	Medicine Religious Law Comparative Studies	
1201–1274	Naṣir al-Dīn al-Ṭūsī	Universal Scientific genius
	Mathematics Astronomy Philosophy	The Ṭūsī Couple
		Saved libraries from Halagu (Observatory at Maragha)
		New planetary models
1236–1311	Quṭb al-Dīn al-Shīrāzī	Commentaries on Canon of Ibn Sīna
	Medicine (optics) Mathematics (Geometry) Astronomy/Geography Philosophy	Encyclopedic works on Astrophysics

PERIOD	SCIENTIST	REMARKS
1332—1406	Abd al-Raḥmān ibn Khaldūn	*Kitāb al-Ibar*
	Philosophy and science of history (Historiography) Psychology Father of social sciences	History of North Africa *Al-Muqaddimah* Rise and fall of cultures Contemporaries Kashānī *Qazizadah* (trigonometry: value of pi) Observatory at Samarqand Busti, Maridini
1546–1621	Bahā'uddīn al-ʿAmilī	Shaykh al-Islam Applications of Mathematics &
	Mathematics, Chemistry Architecture Religious Sciences	Geometry to architecture Decimal fractions Contemporaries: Yazdī & Isfahānī

6

Contributions of Muslim Physicians and Other Scholars: 700-1600 AC

M. BASHEER AHMED

INTRODUCTION

PRIOR TO THE ADVENT of Islam, Arabic society was uncivilized, ignorant, barbarous, and showed little interest in intellectual matters. The Qur'an was revealed to the Prophet Muhammad during the years 612–632 as a book of guidance, and this had a profound effect on Arab society. The first revelation of the Qur'an inspired the Prophet of Islam to acquire knowledge and emphasized the importance of learning in human life. The Qur'an repeatedly urges humankind to understand the forces of nature for the benefit of human beings and their intellectual growth, and it has brought to humanity an interest in scientific thinking.

> Proclaim! And your Lord is Most Bountiful. He Who taught [the use of] the pen. Taught man that which he knew not. (96:3–5)

The Qur'an makes it clear that all that is in the heavens and in the earth has been made subservient to human beings, the vicegerents of Allah. Allah has endowed human beings with the capacity to use their intellect to reflect upon things, and to express their ideas in speech and writing (55:1–4).[1] Muslims are encouraged by the commandments of the Qur'an and the Prophetic Sayings to seek knowledge, and study nature to see the signs of the Creator, which thus inspires human intellectual growth. This was the main reason why Muslims made contributions to scientific development. In another verse the Qur'an urges the reader to think, investigate, and find out the mysteries of the world.

> Do they not look at the camels, how they were created? The heaven, how it
> was raised high? The mountains, how they were firmly set? And the earth,
> how it was spread out? So keep on giving admonition, for you are an
> admonisher ... (88:17–21)

Qur'anic verses encourage man to reflect (think) and understand the
nature God created.

> In the earth there are tracks side by side, gardens of grapes, corn fields, and
> palm trees; growing out of single roots or otherwise. They are all watered
> with the same water, yet we make some of them excel others in taste.
> Surely in this there are signs for people who use their common sense.
> (13:4)

There are hundreds of similar verses in the Qur'an which describe the
mysteries of the universe and stimulate human thinking toward understanding and exploring the laws of nature. The Qur'an emphasizes the
need for the observation of natural processes and the reflection upon on
what has been observed. No verse in the Qur'an contradicts scientific data.
Thus, theology, philosophy, and science are finally harmonized by Islam's
ability to reconcile religion and science.[2] According to the Sayings of
Prophet Muhammad, "there is no illness without a cure" and since Allah
has created a cure for all diseases except old age, it is necessary for scientists to search for the cure of diseases by advances in medical treatment.
The following Prophetic traditions highlight the importance of seeking
knowledge:

> The search for knowledge is obligatory on every Muslim or Muslimah.
> The ink of Scholars is worth more than the blood of martyrs.
> He who adores knowledge, adores God.
> Wisdom is the goal of all believers, acquire it from anyone.
> Whoever wishes to have the benefit of this world, let him acquire
> knowledge. Whoever wishes to have the benefit of the world hereafter, let
> him acquire knowledge.[3]

Prophet Muhammad further pointed out that only the learned would
inherit his legacy, and would be the trustees of Allah on earth. He is said
to have encouraged Muslims to travel to China if necessary in search of
knowledge. Muslims should not regard the worldly sciences as discouraged or forbidden. The Prophet says: "Whoever goes in search of know-

ledge is in the path of Allah till he returns," and "Allah makes easy the path of Paradise to him who journeys for the sake of knowledge."[4] Obviously, when the Prophet emphasized traveling in search of knowledge, he was not referring only to the knowledge of the Qur'an and Shari'ah, which was readily available in Makkah and Madinah. Therefore, during the early period of Islam, Muslims had a better and deeper understanding of the Qur'an and Prophetic guidance and took it upon themselves to go all over the world to seek knowledge and to establish fine institutions of learning throughout the Muslim world. The new methods of experimentation, observation, and measurement on which modern science is based are all contributions of those who followed the true teachings of Islam.[5]

The pre-Islamic Arabs had little knowledge of the physical and experimental sciences. It was only after the conquest of Egypt and some territories of the Byzantine Empire that the Muslims came across some scientific institutions in Jundaishapura, Harran, and Alexandria. There they discovered the scientific and philosophical works of the Greeks, which aroused their curiosity and the desire to acquire knowledge.[6] The period between the eighth and fourteenth centuries is regarded as the Golden Age in Muslim history, during which the Muslims established the most powerful empire and produced the most brilliant scientists and scholars of that time. Muslim scholars such as Ibn Sīnā, al-Khawārizmī, al-Rāzī, al-Zahrāwī, al-Bayūnī, Ibn al-Haytham, al-Idrīsī, al-Kindī, Ibn Khaldūn and hundreds of other Muslim scientists made their observations and original research and added a vast treasure of scientific knowledge to mathematics, medical sciences, astronomy, geography, economics, and philosophy. The contributions of Muslim scientists and scholars show the highest quality of scientific development during that period. Muslim scientists were distributed throughout the Muslim empire from Bukhara (Uzbekistan) in the east to Baghdad (Iraq), Isfahan (Iran) and Córdoba (Andalusia – Spain) in the West. They established universities and learning centers that attracted students from all over the world. Córdoba alone contained 17 universities, 70 public libraries and hundreds of thousands of books for students.[7]

Muslim scholars, under the guidance of the Qur'an and Sunnah, which encouraged scientific exploration of the world as a form of worship, produced excellent scientific and other scholarly works that eventually had a profound influence on Western thought, and Western civilization. This

was during the time of the West's Dark Ages, in which the entire intellectu-
alism of Church dogma suppressed scientific progress. The Church opposed freedom of thought, and even a great scientist such as Galileo was
punished for his theory that the earth rotates around the sun, which
clashed with the Church's dogma. For a thousand years, scientific, medical, and scholarly work virtually stopped in Europe. Most of the work
done by Greeks and some Roman scholars remained dormant. The burning of the great library of Alexandria in 390 AC by fundamentalist Christians had already resulted in the loss of valuable works.[8]

Unfortunately, the West has continually suppressed and downplayed
the contributions of Muslim scientists. Most books and articles on the
history of medicine and the sciences outline the contribution of Greek
scientists, which is usually followed by the scientific progress since the
Renaissance. Students are taught that Christian European scientists made
all the scientific advances after the original Greek contributions. The
scholarly work of Muslim scientists is rarely acknowledged in major
publications of medical and scientific works in the West. Morowitz, a
historian, described this phenomenon of concealment as "History's Black
Hole." "This is [a] myth that gives a distorted view by giving the impression that [the] Renaissance arose Pheonix-like from ashes, smoldering for a millennium of classical age of Greece and Rome."[9]

Nevertheless, a number of distinguished historians and scientific
investigators (like John Williams, E.A. Myers, Max Meyerhof, Philip K.
Hitti, George Sarton, M. Ullman, E.G. Brown and Savage Smith) have
fully acknowledged the part played by medieval Muslim scientists not
only in preserving the knowledge of Ancient Greece, Persia, and India,
but also adding original contributions to the wealth of knowledge.[10]
Bernard Lewis further clarifies in his book on the Middle East that Islamic
scientific development was not solely dependent on ancient Greek
knowledge:

> [T]he achievement of medieval Islamic science is not limited to the preser-
> vation of Greek learning, nor to the incorporation in the corpus of elements
> from the more ancient and more distant East. This heritage which medieval
> Islamic scientists handed on to the modern world was immensely enriched
> by their own efforts and contributions. Greek science on the whole rather
> tended to be speculative and theoretical. Medieval Middle Eastern science
> was much more practical and in such fields as medicine, chemistry, astron-

omy, and agronomy, the classical heritage was clarified and supplemented by the experiments and observations of the medieval Middle East.[11]

The output, originality, and creativity in science and technology in the Muslim world continued until about the sixteenth century. During this period, Muslim scientific and scholarly works gradually spread to Europe.[12] Sicily and Spain were the principal centers of such dissemination. From Spain the knowledge penetrated beyond the Pyrenees into western and south-western France and Sicily. The Christian ruler, Roger II, was instrumental in spreading Muslim scientific contributions and culture throughout Italy and across the Alps to various European cities, which themselves became centers of Arab learning.

This chapter aims to contribute to a more accurate understanding of the history of medicine and the sciences by focusing on the contributions that Muslim scientists made during the Muslim "Golden Age."

Within two centuries of the death of Prophet Muhammad, the Muslims had conquered new lands, and their empire extended from India in the East to Spain in the West, including Arabia, Syria, Egypt, Iraq, North Africa, Iran, and Turkey. These isolated nations now became part of the Muslim empire. As a result, Muslims were introduced to different languages and scientific technological advances from various civilizations of the world. Muslim scholars and businessmen traveled to other distant places, like India and China, and brought back knowledge with them. In addition to a geographical unity of Asian, African, and European countries, Arabic became an international language facilitating communications across different cultures and regions, and it also became a language of science and technology.

Islam's tolerance and encouragement of both secular and religious learning, created the necessary climate for the free exchange and propagation of ideas and knowledge. Baghdad and Córdoba became the world's greatest learning and teaching centers. All the available scientific works on mathematics, philosophy, medicine, and astronomy were translated from the languages of Greece, Rome, India, Persia, and Syria into Arabic. The Abbasid Caliphs, who were recognized for their pursuit of knowledge and support of academics, established the *Bayt al-Ḥikmah* (House of Wisdom) and sent emissaries to various parts of the world, including the Byzantine Empire, to collect scientific manuscripts. Caliph al-Ma'mūn established a school of translation and appointed Ḥunayn ibn

Isḥāq, a Christian, as the Director, who was a gifted translator and scientist. Ḥunayn ibn Isḥāq did major translations of the entire works of Aristotle, Hypocrites, and Galen into Arabic. The *Bayt al-Ḥikmah* had a long-lasting influence on mathematics, economics, astronomy and philosophy, chemistry, and the medical sciences. It produced famous Muslim thinkers such as al-Kindī and al-Fārābī. Caliph al-Muhtadi (ninth century) patronized another scholar, Thābit ibn Qurrah (a Sabian), who translated and published commentaries on the works of famous Greek scientists and philosophers and published some original work on mathematics, astronomy, and philosophy. Sinān, son of Thābit ibn Qurrah became the Director of several hospitals (*bimaristans*) in Baghdad.

The Spanish Umayyad Caliphs' liberal support for academic work also played an important role in producing original scientific works. "The world is held up by four pillars: the wisdom of the learned, the justice of the great, the prayers of the righteous, and the valor of the brave" was the inscription often found at the entrance of universities in Spain during the Muslim era.[13] In Spain, the participation of non-Muslim scholars in the scientific enterprises also shows the admirable quality of interfaith tolerance and cooperation adopted by the Umayyad Caliphs.

Commenting on the rise of Islamic civilization and its policy of tolerance towards people of all faiths, John Esposito points out:

> The genesis of Islamic civilization was indeed a collaborative effort, incorporating the learning and wisdom of many cultures and languages. As in government administration, Christians and Jews who had been the intellectual and bureaucratic backbone of the Persian and Byzantine empires participated in the process as well as Muslims. This ecumenical effort was evident in Caliph al-Maʿmūn's reign. The House of Wisdom's translation center was headed by the renowned scholar, Ḥunayn ibn Isḥāq, a Nestorian Christian. This period of translation was followed by the original contributions of Muslim intellectuals and their artistic activity. Muslims ceased to be disciples and became masters, in the process of producing Islamic civilization dominated by the Arabic language and Islam's view of life.[14]

Unfortunately, this aspect of Islamic tolerance is not recognized in the West today. The Arabic translations of important treatises from Greek, Indian, and other pre-Islamic civilizations preserved precious works for thousands of years and prevented their extinction. Many translations, along with Arabic commentaries were translated again into Latin and re-introduced into Europe. These translations and the original contributions of Muslim scientists and scholars became the foundation of modern medical and other sciences.[15] Muslim physicians established medical schools in Baghdad and Córdoba where students from the Middle East and Europe came to study. The European medical schools of Montpellier, Padua, and Pisa were founded on the pattern of Muslim medical schools in Córdoba. The medical encyclopedic work, 'al-Qānūn' of Ibn Sīnā (The Canon of Avicenna), and the books on surgery by Abū al-Qāsim al-Zahrāwī remained the textbooks of medical sciences through-out Europe until the sixteenth century, when European works came to replace these texts.[16]

Greek scientists were excellent at theorizing and formulating hypotheses. They were great observers, but not experimentalists. Greek literature did not show any documentation of experiments. Muslim scientists, for the first time in history, introduced the concept of the recording of data based on both observation and experimentation. The Greeks had a strong belief that Aristotle and Plato's opinions were final and that there was no possibility of mistakes in their views, although they were only theorizing and attempting to explain various phenomena to the best of the capabilities of their speculative knowledge.[17] As Briffault wrote,

> Science owes a great deal more to the Arab culture, it owes its existence to Arab scientists, who made startling discoveries and revolutionary theories. The Greeks systematized, generalized, and theorized, but the patient ways of investigation, the accumulation of positive knowledge, the minute methods of science, detailed, prolonged observation, and experimental inquiry were introduced to the European world by Arabs only.[18]

I turn now to elaborate on some more specific contributions to medicine, chemistry, pharmacology, mathematics, astronomy, geography, political science, sociology, philosophy, and technology.

MEDICAL SCIENCES

The major well-researched scientific progress in medicine was made between the eighth and eleventh centuries, during the Umayyad and

Abbasid eras. Muslims became acquainted with Greek anatomical descriptions, and from their own research, found many errors in their
work. For instance, in opposition to Galen, who thought that the human
skull consisted of seven bones, the Muslim scholars held that it had
Muḥammad found that there were ossicles in the ear, which facilitate
hearing.[19] Yuhanna ibn Massawaih dissected a monkey to acquire more
information about the human body. Al-Zahrāwī emphasized that the
knowledge of anatomy was necessary to become a surgeon.

From the ninth to the twelfth century, many great hospitals were built.
These hospitals were called *bimaristan* (*bimar* – sick, *stan* – a place to
stay). They were well-organized institutions based on the principles of
human dignity, honor, and hygiene. They were well administered by com-
petent physicians, and also served as teaching hospitals and research institutions. Many famous Muslim physicians were attached to these hospitals. One of the early hospitals, Muqtadī, was founded in Baghdad in
916 under the direction of a famous physician, al-Rāzī. This hospital
retained several physicians on the staff, including specialists like surgeons
and bone-setters (orthopedic surgeons). The development of these hospitals was an outstanding contribution by Muslim physicians. The hospitals served all citizens free of charge and irrespective of race or religion.
There were separate units for male and female patients, and special wards
for medical diseases, contagious diseases, and psychiatric patients. The
physicians and nursing staff were licensed to assure quality of care.
Libraries were also affiliated to the hospitals, which were frequently used
by students and teachers. It is recorded that these hospitals were furnished
like palaces. Ibn Jubayr, the renowned Arab traveler described the care
for the patients in Muqtadī Hospital as follows:

> In this hospital, the best arrangements exist for providing medical aid. The
> patients are dealt with very courteously and sympathetically. All patients
> are given food and care freely. For meeting the sanitary requirements, the
> water of the Tigris is supplied through pipes. Every Monday and Thursday
> eminent medical consultants visit this hospital and assist the regular staff
> in diagnosing complicated and chronic diseases, and suggesting their
> treatment. In addition, medical attendants prepare food and medicine for
> every patient under the guidance of the medical men treating him.[20]

In major cities like Baghdad, the mentally ill were treated in separate hospitals. The first known hospital for the mentally ill was built in the tenth century in Baghdad, and later in Damascus. The mentally ill patients were treated with kindness and dignity, and their suffering was recognized as part of the illness. This was the period when the mentally ill were regarded as "witches and "possessed" in Europe, and some of them were burned alive. In contrast, the mentally ill patients in hospitals of Baghdad received medication and support services. It was not until 1793 that Philippe Pinel introduced humane treatment for the mentally ill in France, which was adopted elsewhere in Europe at a later date.

Muslim physicians initiated the regulation of medical practice the licensing of physicians and pharmacologists. Similar rules were later established in Sicily, when Roger II, King of Sicily (1095–1154), established the requirement of passing an examination before a physician could start practicing medicine. Thus the requirement of licensing began in Europe in Italy, followed by Spain and France.

From the European medical schools at Montpellier and Salerno, this vast medical knowledge was disseminated throughout Europe. The *Pharmacopoeia* of the London College of Physicians (1618), a classic work systematizing drugs, recognized this debt to Muslim (and Greek) physicians and contains illustrations of the portraits of a few of these great scholars: Hypocrites; Galen; Avicenna (Ibn Sīna); and Mesuë (Ibn Zakariyyah bin Masawayh).[21]

Muslim surgeons developed a number of surgical techniques that were extremely advanced, especially in eye surgery. They used cauterization extensively in surgery, and described a variety of illnesses that were treated by cauterization. Ibn Zuhr (twelfth century) described how to perform a tracheotomy, and al-Zahrāwī (tenth century) invented many surgical instruments, such as those for the internal examination of the inner ear, the inspection of urethra, and an instrument for the removal of foreign bodies from the throat. His books on surgery contained illustrations of all the surgical instruments that he was using. Muslim physicians also made use of anesthetic substances while performing operations.

Muslim physicians were the first to write medical textbooks in a format that medical students could use in their studies. These textbooks were based on original Greek and other existing works and also new scientific data gathered by the Muslim physicians themselves. The most famous medical scholarly works were produced by al-Rāzī (Rhazes, 932), al-Zahrāwī (Albucasis, 1013) and Ibn Sīna (Avicenna, 1092). Al-Rāzī was the first physician to describe how to differentiate between measles and smallpox. He also discussed the treatment of various ailments by dietary restriction and regulation. After several centuries, we are once again including dietary regulation as the most important part of treatment for a number of severe illnesses like diabetes, hypertension, and heart disease. Al-Rāzī's textbooks were translated into Latin and used in European medical schools until the sixteenth century. Ibn Sīna's encyclopedic work, *Qānūn Fī al-Ṭib*, surveyed the entire medical knowledge available from ancient and Muslim sources. He also documented his original contributions such as the recognition of the contagious nature of pthisis and tuberculosis, and the spread of diseases through water and soil. His books contained an authentic record of 760 drugs that were in use, and his writings were translated and used as textbooks for medicine for several centuries in Europe.

Al-Rāzī along with Ibn Sīna described the different parts of the eye and noted that the movement of the eyeball was caused by contractions of eye muscles, and pupilary movements were caused by contractions and expansions of the iris. Muslim surgeons also performed operations for the removal of cataracts. Ibn al-Haytham's (956–1038) most important contribution was a correct explanation of visual perception. He was the first to prove that rays passed from objects toward the eyes, not vice versa, which was the prevalent belief postulated by Euclid and Ptolemy. He also described how the impressions of objects made upon the eye are conveyed along the optic nerve to the brain, culminating in the formation of visual images.[22]

Abū al-Qāsim al-Zahrāwī was born in Córdoba in 936 and he is considered the greatest surgeon, whose comprehensive medical text combining Eastern and classical teachings shaped European surgical procedures until the Renaissance. He wrote famous books including: *al-Tasrīf* in 30 volumes, which contained the work of previous surgeons and his own surgical procedures. The last part of the book, containing drawings of more than 200 instruments, constituted the first illustrated independent work on surgery. His books remained the leading authority on surgery for 500 years in Europe.[23]

Muslim physicians described the anatomy of the lung and bronchi and the interactions between the human body's bloodvessels and air in the lungs. Ibn al-Nafīs (1213–1288) was the first to describe the two circulatory systems, namely, aortic and pulmonary, three centuries before Harvey's discovery. He also elaborated on the function of coronary arteries in supplying the heart muscle.

CHEMISTRY

Muslims developed chemistry as a distinct branch of science, and the word "chemistry" is derived from the Arabic word *al-kīmiyah*. It needs to be pointed out that Muslim scientists who pioneer work in chemistry are often called al-chemists, and sometimes *al-kīmiyah* is associated with a pseudo-science concerned with the transmutation of base metal into gold. *Al* in Arabic means "the," and *kīmiyah* means chemistry; therefore, the word *al-kīmiyah* means "the chemistry" and should not be confused with pseudo sciences.[24] The most notable Muslim scientists opposed the false notion that ordinary metals could be changed into gold by a chemical process. The eighth-century Muslim scientist from Iraq, Jābbir ibn Ḥayyān (Geber), is known as the Father of Chemistry. He was the first scientist to introduce experimental investigation (*tajribah*) into chemistry by perfecting techniques of crystalization, distilation, sublimation, and evaporation, developing several instruments to perform these tests. He also discovered several minerals and acids, which he prepared for the first time. Jābir described three distinct types of substances: spirit, those which vaporize with heat as camphor and ammonium chloride; metals such as gold, silver, and iron; and compounds which can be converted into powder. He wrote over 2,000 papers on his experimental work. Jābbir ibn Ḥayyān advised his students not to accept anything as true until they had examined it themselves. "The most important task of the al-Chemist is to do practical work and to carry out experiments. Without practical appli-cation and experiment, nothing can be achieved."[25]

David Tschnaz stated that Jābir's works on al-chemy (chemistry) were translated into Latin and made their way into Europe. For centuries they served as the ultimate authority to European scientists including Arnold of Villanova (1240–1313), Roger Bacon (1214–1294) and Albert Magnus (1193–1280). In this process, many of the basic terms of chemistry and pharmacology, for example, alkali syrup, julep, and alchemy (*kīmiyah*) itself were introduced into European languages – a testimony to the wide-ranging contribution of these early Arab scientists.[26]

Al-Rāzī, one of the greatest Muslim physicians of the ninth century, was also a brilliant chemist who continued his work on chemistry while practicing as a physician. He refined the processes of distillation and sublimation. He also introduced mercurial compounds for the treatment of various ailments. Ibn Sīna, another brilliant scientist, also adopted Ibn Jābir's methods for chemical experimentation, and used them as the basis for determining the efficacy of new pharmaceuticals.

Gustave Le Bon, the French Orientalist, attributes modern European chemistry to Muslim scientists:

> It must be remembered that no sign, either of chemistry, or any other science, was discovered all of a sudden. The Arabs had established 1,000 years ago their laboratories in which they used to conduct scientific experiments and publish their discoveries without which Lavoisier [called the father of chemistry] would not have been able to produce anything in this field. It can be said without the fear of contradiction, that owing to researches and experiments by Muslim Scientists, modern chemistry came into being, and that it produced great results in the form of great scientific inventions.[27]

PHARMACOLOGY

Muslim physicians also made the most significant contributions in pharmacology. They not only discovered many herbal drugs but also perfected many of the techniques of chemical extraction, including distillation, sublimation, filtration, coagulation, and crystallization owing to their expertise in chemistry. Al-Zahāwī (936–1035), a prominent surgeon who was very skilled in the use of simple and compound remedies, was known as a pharmacist surgeon. The thirteenth-century Muslim Spanish scientist, al-Bayṭār, visited Africa, India, and Europe and collected samples of plants through extensive field studies. He classified plants in alphabetical order according to their characteristics and therapeutic qualities. He also recorded the Arabic, Latin, and Berber names of the plants and included information about the preparation of drugs and their administration. He discovered and documented 200 new plants that had not been known previously. His famous book, *Kitāb al-Jāmiᶜ Fī al-Adwiyah al-Mufradah*, (A Compendium of Simple Drugs and Foods) was translated into Latin and was used in the formulation of the first London Pharmacopoeia issued by the College of Physicians during the reign of King James I.[28]

According to Levey, the Muslims were expert organizers of knowledge, and their pharmacological texts were carefully organized in a way that was useful to the apothecary and medical practitioner.[29]

MATHEMATICS

Muslims made numerous discoveries in the field of mathematics, which have been passed on to modern science, contributing to the technological revolution of early modern Europe. One of the most notable of these innovations was the concept of zero. Al-Khawārizmī, a Persian scholar living in the ninth century, was appointed as a scientist in the *Bayt al-Ḥikmah* of Baghdad by the Caliph. He developed the concept of algorithms – a method of calculation – which bears the anglicized version of its inventor's name. His work in algebra was outstanding, for he gave analytical solutions to linear and quadratic equations, which established him as the Father of Algebra. The word "algebra" is derived from his famous book, *al-Jabr wa al-Muqābalah* (The Compendium of Calculation by Completion and Balancing). The book contained the most important aspects of al-Khawārizmī's work. and is generally considered the first to have been written on the subject. Al-Khawārizmī also learned the concept of zero from India, and it was transmitted in his works to Europe. The Indians had left a blank for a zero, and al-Khawārizmī's addition was to give it a symbol, the "0." Even the English word "zero" is derived from the Arabic name for this symbol ṣifr. Leonardo Da Vinci studied the Arabic numeral system and introduced it to Europe.[30]

Abū al-Wafā al-Buzjānī (940–997) developed trigonometry. He was the first person to show the generality of the sine theorem relative to spherical triangles.[31] Al-Ṭūsī, another Muslim scientist of the thirteenth century, developed spherical trigonometry, including 6 fundamental formulas for the solution of spherical, right-angled triangles.

ASTRONOMY

A Muslim astronomer of the tenth century, al-Battani made several original contributions to the study of astronomy. He determined the solar year as being of 365 days, 4 hrs, and 46 minutes. He proposed a new and ingenious theory to determine the visibility of the new moon. European astronomers used his observations of solar eclipses in 1749 to determine the acceleration of the motion of the moon.

Muslims invented the compass and al-Farganī (860) estimated the circumference of the earth to be 24,000 miles. Muslims were the first to use the pendulum, build observatories, catalog the maps of the visible stars, and correct the sun and moon tables. They also wrote about sunspots, eclipses, and comets. Muslim scientists made a distinction between astronomy and astrology, and regarded astrology as a pseudoscience. The thirteenth-century Muslim astronomer, al-Ṭūsī, earned his fame by producing astronomical tables called *al-Zij Ilkhanī*, which became the most popular tables among astronomers. He pointed out several serious shortcomings in Ptolemy's astronomy, and foreshadowed the later dissatisfaction with the system that culminated in the Copernican reforms. In the tenth century, Muslims built an observatory in Baghdad and the famous Samarqand observatory was built in the thirteenth century when al-Ṭūsī worked on the measurements of planetary movements. Ibn Shaitar of Damascus (fourteenth century) continued the work on planetary movements, using a combination of perfect circulatory motions. The famous European astronomer, Copernicus, was familiar with Ibn Shaiṭar's work and used his theories to suggest a hectocenteric system of movements of planets, as opposed to Ptolemy's geocenteric system.[33]

GEOGRAPHY

Al-Masʿūdī, a tenth-century Muslim geographer and historian, traveled to Baghdad, India, China, and several other countries of the world. He described his experiences as well as the people, climates, and the geography and history of the various countries that he visited. He documented historical events chronologically and wrote 34 books covering a variety of these subjects. Al-Bayrūnī, another great Muslim scholar of the eleventh century from Uzbekistan, was famous for his world travels, which he also recorded in a graphic account of the history and societies of the people that he encountered. He translated many books from the Indian language, Sanskrit, into Arabic, thus introducing the work of Indian scholars to Muslim scholars. Al-Idrīsī, a twelfth-century Muslim geographer from Southern Spain, studied in Córdoba and traveled widely in Spain, North Africa, Anatolia, and Europe. He settled in Sicily and wrote one of the greatest books of descriptive geography: *Kitāb Nuzuhāt al-Mushtāq Fī Ikhtrāq al-Āfāq* (The Pleasures of Travel by One who is Eager to Traverse the Regions of the World). Al-Idrīsī described the people and the customs, as well as the distance between the major cities, and the products and climates of the entire known world. He prepared a silver plainsphere on which a map of the world was depicted. He also wrote extensively on medicinal plants.[34]

POLITICAL SCIENCE

Although less is known about this aspect in the West, Muslim scholars have contributed to the development of political science and defined the role of politics in Islam, where there is no separation of State and Church. Al-Māwardī was a political scientist of the eleventh century and was a great jurist, sociologist, and expert on the subject. He discussed the principles of political science with special references to the functions of Caliphs, the Chief Minister, other ministers, and the relationship between various elements of the public and a government. He laid down clear principles for the election of Caliphs and criticized the established practice by asserting that Sharicah (Islamic Law) by itself was an insufficient yardstick for justice. His greatest contribution was the introduction of political justice into Sharicah.[35]

SOCIOLOGY

Ibn Khaldūn, a fourteenth-century Muslim sociologist wrote *Muqaddimah* [Introduction], the first volume of world history, which gave him a special place among historians, sociologists, and philosophers. He documented the psychological, economic, environmental, and social factors that contributed to the advancement of human civilization. He postulated the theory of cyclical change in human civilization caused by dynamically changing social, economic, political, and geographical factors. His writings on the development of history in its totality gave rise to a new discipline, that of social science. As a historiographer, and a philosopher of the science of history, he has had no equal so far in any age or country.[36]

PHILOSOPHY

The Muslim philosophers admired the work of Greek philosophers, Plato and Aristotle, wrote commentaries on their works, and made original contributions. Al-Kindī, (ninth century) was one of the early Muslim philosophers who was distinguished as the "Philosopher of the Arabs." He explained that philosophy did not conflict with religion, and could

give one a deeper understanding of the religion (Islam). Al-Fārābī, an
Andalusian Muslim philosopher of the tenth century, built his arguments
on abstract knowledge and founded a Neoplatonic school in Islamic
philosophy. He wrote a book on a model city similar to that of Plato's
Republic though conceived within the Islamic framework. He also made
the study of logic easier by dividing it into two categories: *Takhayyul*
(idea) and *Thubūt* (proof). The eleventh-century Muslim philosopher and
theologian, al-Ghazālī, was the dean of the Niẓāmiyyah University in
Baghdad; he portrayed the inability of reason to comprehend the Absolute, the Infinite and further elaborated that an infinite time is related to
infinite space. He was able to create a balance between religion and
reason, identifying their respective spheres as being the infinite, and the
finite respectively. The twelfth-century Spanish Muslim philosopher, Ibn
Rushd, was regarded as the greatest rationalist of his age. He was a great
exponent of the harmony of philosophy and religion, stating: "Man is
neither in full control of his destiny, nor is it fully predetermined for him."
He also promoted the idea that philosophy did not conflict with Islam,
and supported rationalism by quoting verses of the Qur'an. Ibn Rushd's
philosophy influenced the thirteenth-century Christian philosopher,
St. Thomas Aquinas. He was credited with building the greatest Catholic
system of thought that has ever been offered. He synthesized the
philosophy of Aristotle, the theory of St. Augustine, and the philosophy
of al-Ghazālī and Ibn Rushd. In his famous work, *Summa Theologica*, he
followed al-Ghazālī's *'Iḥyā' ʿUlūm al-Dīn'* (Revival of the Sciences of
Religion) and developed an understanding of the relationship between
philosophy and faith. His understanding of the harmony between religion
and natural sciences derived from the high culture of Islamic Spain and
Ibn Rushd's philosophical writings. Another thirteenth-century Spanish
Muslim philosopher, Ibn al-ʿArabī, incorporated many fragmented and
mono-systematic mystic doctrines into a system, and gave an explicit
theoretical formulation. His work, *Fuṣūṣ al-Ḥikam*, was regarded as a
masterpiece of mystic thought in Sufism. Another renowned Muslim
philosopher of the thirteenth century, Rūmī, is well known to the West.
His famous book, *Mathnawī*, offers solutions to many complicated
problems in metaphysics, religion, ethics, and mysticism. He explains
various hidden aspects of Sufism and their relationship with worldly
life.[37]

TECHNOLOGY

Muslim contributions to technology were equally superb. The landmark contribution was the introduction of paper, the knowledge of which had been acquired from China. Muslims established paper factories in Samarqand and later in Baghdad and Syria.[38] During the eighth and ninth centuries, these mills were built all over the Muslim world from Spain to Iran. In contrast, the first paper factory in Europe was established as late as the late thirteenth century. The replacement of parchment and papyrus with paper had a profound effect on the spread and democratization of education, for it became possible to write books and to preserve and distribute knowledge more easily. In some Middle Eastern schools in the ninth century, it was available free of charge. Syria also established glass-making factories, producing glassware and pottery of high quality. This technique of glass manufacturing was transferred to Venice in the twelfth century. Venice still produces the finest glasswork in the world.

Muslims made advances in the fabric, silk, cotton, and leather industries. During the ninth and tenth centuries, hundreds of ships from Muslim countries docked at the port of Canton in China. Muslim traders established a system of letters of credit similar to checks. They worked with all kinds of metal, for example, gold, silver, bronze, iron, and steel. Muslims practiced farming in the scientific way and knew the value of fertilizers.[39] In the twelfth century, Muslim agriculture, irrigation, and manufacture of farm equipment were far more advanced than those of non-Muslim Europe. This advanced technology was later transferred from Spain to Italy and Northern Europe.[40] Philip Hitti writes,

> During all the first part of the Middle Ages, no other people made as important contributions to human progress, as did the Arabs. From 9th to 12th century, there were more philosophical, medical, historical, astronomical, and geographic works written in Arabic than in any other language of the world.[41]

CONCLUSION

This chapter has highlighted Muslim scientists' contributions to civilization. Unfortunately, these contributions gradually declined, and came to a halt owing to a rapid loss of political power, and a marked lack of inspiration for education and technological achievement.

When southern Spain was conquered by Ferdinand in 1490, hundreds of thousands of Arabic volumes of scientific discourses were burned. The Spanish government went to extraordinary lengths to prohibit the possession of any book written in Arabic by Muslim scholars except those which had been translated into Latin. In the thirteenth century, Mongol armies burned valuable books written by Muslim scholars in Baghdad, and in the twelfth and thirteenth centuries, the Crusaders destroyed many Muslim scientific works in Syria.

Many non-Muslims translated the original works of Muslim scholars and Latinized the Muslim names. In subsequent years, Europeans failed to recognize that Muslim scholars had done the original work on which current scientific progress had been made. Anti-Muslim prejudice has also played an important role in the loss of recognition of Muslim scientists and their scholarly work.

Although the production of scientific work and knowledge by Muslim scholars was brought to a halt owing to the factors mentioned above, the scientific progress that they had generated continued. Major scientific works of Muslims were translated from Arabic to Latin, and Christians in Europe learned medicine, chemistry, physics, mathematics, and philosophy from the books written by Muslim scholars. Many European students graduated from the famous Muslim universities of Córdoba, Toledo, Baghdad, and Damascus, and returned to Europe to establish and teach in the newer universities. In many European schools, the Arabic language as well as Latin became the medium of instruction. New medical schools were established in Europe, teaching the same curriculum as that of Muslim Spain and Baghdad. The textbooks written by Muslim scholars were translated into Latin, and remained a major source of learning until the sixteenth century.

The major reason for the decline in scientific achievement in the Muslim world was the Muslims' gradual loss of interest in scientific subjects. Two parallel systems of education were developed, namely Shariʿah – the science of Islamic jurisprudence, and al-ʿUlūm al-ʿAqliyyah – the natural sciences and technology. Most scientific theories such as the theory of evolution were recognized as anti-religious and many Muslims turned away from modern sciences. The decline in progress continued owing to apathy toward scientific discoveries. The schools (Madāris) refrained from teaching the more advanced courses of mathematics, science, and philosophy, focusing instead on the theological, spiritual, and ritualistic aspects of Islam and Islamic Law (*Shariʿah*). There was an overall demoralization in the new Muslim generation to acquire new knowledge and to do scientific research. Commenting on religious fanaticism, narrow-mindedness and a lack of tolerance, Manzoor Alam states:

> The transfer of science and technology from the Islamic realm to Europe was followed by a sharp decline of the political power of Islam, and the rise of fanaticism in Islam dealt a mortal blow to the development of science. It is symbolized by the destruction of the Istanbul Astronomical Observatory in 1580 by the fanatics which was established by Taqiyuddīn in 1545. The rise of the clerics and fanaticism stifled the growth of science in the countries ruled by Muslim rulers such as the Mooghul [Moghul] Empire in India, Ottoman Empire in Turkey and Arabia and smaller kingdoms in the Maghrib. The language barrier re-emerged forcefully since most of the post 16th century scientific researches were conducted in Spanish, German, Italian, French, and English languages. Hence the language of science and technology once again became inaccessible to Muslims all over the world and consequently the Muslim countries rapidly lapsed into decay.[42]

One wonders about the possible shape of the world today if Muslim scientists had been able to continue their research and scholarly work.

Today, Muslims are seriously under-represented in science. Less than one percent of the world's scientists are Muslim, whereas 25 percent of the world's population are Muslim. Muslims have developed a false perception that all knowledge is in the Qur'an. Most conservative Muslims discourage the study of science, regarding it as "Western." Many conservative imams discourage rational questioning and innovation. Nevertheless, to become a scientist, it is essential to have the ability to think critically and to have an inquisitive mind. A scientist's work is dependent on thinking, developing a hypothesis, experimenting, and recording the observations. Thus, science and technology (*ʿIlm al-Ḥikmah*) have been transferred from the East to the West. Science does not belong to a particular ethnic or religious group. It is a never-ending evolution that will continue to occur with contributions from different races and groups at different times.

After 400 years of stagnation, the Muslim community is now re-awakening and seeking its lost identity. We are reviewing and learning about the contributions of Muslim scholars to science and civilization.

We are taking a pride in the scientific work of Muslim scientists. We are now recognizing our responsibilities to correct the erroneous notion that modern civilization and scientific advancement are a creation exclusive to a particular culture or civilization.

The new generation of Muslim youth will hopefully enhance its self-perception of belonging to a Muslim community that has made a significant impact on world civilization. The progress in science that we are seeing today is like a building to which all nations – both Muslim and non-Muslim, have made their contributions. It is the result of cooperation, communication, and passing on the wealth of information to successive generations from the Greeks to the Muslims to the West, and finally back to the new generation from East and West. Although this brief article on the contributions of Muslim scientists may not fully reflect the work that they have done, it will, nevertheless, serve as an introduction to their scholarly pursuits and accomplishments. However, merely glorifying the past is not enough, for we must continually encourage Muslim youth to become dynamic researchers and follow the path of great Muslim scholars to benefit their fellow human beings everywhere.

7

The Feasibility of an Islamic Economic System in a Modern Economy

MOHAMMED SHARIF

ABSTRACT

This paper examines the feasibility of an Islamic economic system in a modern economy. The contemporary economic system is sophisticated and very complex. Islam established the foundations of its economic system in the seventh century AC and its principles are deemed straightforward and simple. So the question arises: How can such a straight-forward and simple system handle the complicated problems of a modern economy? This is exactly what I intend to answer here using the problems of poverty and inequity as an illustration.

Instead of talking about the problems in the world, however, I will discuss them in the context of the US, simply because this country is the most affluent, technologically the most advanced, and it has all the means at its disposal to eliminate at least the blight of poverty from its economy, although it chronically suffers from it. I will first show the nature of the problems in terms of poverty, hunger, homelessness, lack of medical care, and inequity in the distribution of income and wealth, in stark contradiction to the affluence of the country. Then I will demonstrate how the application of the Islamic principles could, within a very short time, solve these problems without at all stifling the prosperity of the society.

This conclusion, however, should not be misconstrued that Islam cannot deal with the problems of developing countries. During the early days of Islam, Islamic principles worked miraculously to solve these and other problems with the least amount of resources.

INTRODUCTION

THE THEME OF THIS BOOK is the Muslim contributions to civilization. The contribution to economic progress made by the Islamic economic system is an important logical candidate for discussion here, for economic prosperity is one of the prerequisites for achieving scientific development. Given the constraint on space, however, I will limit myself to one important aspect of these contributions – economic justice and human development. I hope that this restricted presentation hopefully will help to clarify the content of my message to readers and so will offer an appreciation of the Islamic economic system in general.

Before delving into the subject, however, I need to describe the fundamental principle of the overall Islamic system, for Islam is not just a religion but a complete way of life and its economic system is only an integral part of the whole. Therefore, this discussion is divided into three stages. First, I will describe the basic Islamic principle of establishing and administering a system – social, economic, or political – and compare it with the basic tenets of contemporary systems. Next, I will deal with the concept of economic progress, distinguishing between growth and development and showing their implications for justice and human development.

The fundamental characteristics of an Islamic economic system will then be listed and their implications examined. Next, I will talk about the problems of poverty and inequity in the United States of America. Finally, I will show how easily the application of Islamic principles can solve these problems without having any adverse effects on economic progress.

FUNDAMENTAL PRINCIPLE OF THE ISLAMIC SYSTEM

The preconditions for the functioning of any system and, more so, for it to make any contribution to civilization, are social and political stability and economic prosperity. There are two alternative ways to achieve these preconditions: imposing participation by coercion or inducing voluntary participation by winning the hearts and minds of the people.

The establishment of an elaborate and complex legal system and the use of strong-arm tactics for its implementation, coupled with a harsh punishment for non-compliance, is the systematic way of forcing participation. In this category, capitalism and communism (socialism) are the two systems dominant in the contemporary world of ideas and practices. The Islamic system provides an alternative that functions and prospers with the dedicated voluntary participation of the members of society.

The fundamental difference between these two systems is their philosophy of how human life should be viewed and treated. The former – both capitalism and communism – consider human life to consist only of a body and a mind. The soul is completely removed from the system, leaving, supposedly, just the individual lives of the people, or its existence and role go completely unrecognized. Since the soul is of no value in society, the economy, and politics, people generally find very little use for it in their individual lives either. The members of this society thus gear themselves toward achieving only material possessions and power and their enjoyment, having little or no moral guidance and no consideration for the needs of the soul. In the absence of any ideal higher than material possessions and power, the Darwinian principle of the survival of the fittest then becomes the sole guiding principle for individuals in their competitive pursuit for material success in life. Under these circumstances, the trampling of the weak by the strong and the concomitant frictions and tensions are logical outcomes. Thus, these materialistic societies find no other option but to institute an elaborate legal system with stringent punishment for its violation and they depend solely on this legal system to maintain stability and insure prosperity. In the absence of any moral code of behavior required for the elevation of the soul (spiritual development), however, individuals generally abide by the law only when there is fear of getting caught. Otherwise, breaking the law for gaining material possessions and power is a common occurrence under these systems.

It is no wonder that although these societies achieve extraordinary material progress, yet they face similarly extraordinary social problems. This contention is illustrated by the high rate of economic growth achieved by state ownership and control in a communist system or by the allocation of most of the resources to a small group of people in a capitalist system to generate the engine of growth with simultaneously enormous costs to society. Society is forced to pay in the form of the loss of individual freedom in a communist system, the creation of extreme inequity in both systems, and generation of chronic poverty in a capitalistic system. While the harsh competition for insatiable material progress leads to intense conflicts of interests, the inequity and poverty generated create the dissatisfaction resulting from the awareness of relative and absolute deprivation. The logical outcome again is a variety of difficult problems for the society to tackle. Society thus responds by enacting more laws, thus complicating the system further and making punishments for non-compliance harsher.

How harsh and stringent the legal system has become to maintain the stability of the social-political-economic system in such a situation can be illustrated by the extent of incarceration in the United States. In the early twenty-first century about seven million people are currently in prison, on probation, and on parole; that is approximately 3 percent of the total population. This method of punishment, however, cannot be said to have reduced crime to any significant extent, although it keeps the system functioning. Nevertheless, it costs $70 billion a year to keep about two million individuals behind bars at the rate of $35,000 per inmate. Note that this is only a fraction of the total cost of running the criminal justice system.

In contrast, Islam maintains social and political stability and attains economic prosperity by establishing an equitable and just system by the dedicated voluntary participation of the members of society. This is achieved, however, not by the threat of law, but by training individual members of society and helping them to develop the best possible human character. In this respect, Islam treats human life, unlike contemporary Western thinking, as consisting of three components – body, mind, and soul. All these three aspects are given equal importance in Islamic philosophy and practice for successful development of a personality with the best of human qualities, and therefore, ultimately, for the efficient functioning of the system. The importance of this balanced development of human life may be understood better by the fact that without the soul (spirit), the body is a piece of dead meat and the mind (represented by the functioning of the brain) is similarly decomposed and non-functioning. The soul, however, does not die: when an individual dies, the soul simply leaves the body and exists as a spirit somewhere in God's universe. While the body and the mind relate to the material aspects of human living, the soul provides the human spirit and thus relates to the spiritual side of human life. Both material and spiritual components comprise the full and complete human life, and therefore, the balanced development of both aspects of life is essential for successful human living.

This balanced development of human personality plays a very important role in the Islamic system in establishing and maintaining social and political stability and achieving economic prosperity, in essence, laying the foundation of Islamic civilization. Islam requires its followers to believe that life on this earth is temporary, that real life starts after death and is infinite, that the individual's deeds in this life will determine the quality of his/her life in the Hereafter, that there is a Day of Judgment after death when the rewards for good deeds and punishment for evil deeds will be handed out by God. More importantly, individuals are accountable to God for their own deeds, God is keeping a complete and perfect record of everything we think, say, and do, and this record will be produced before us at the time of judgment (think of it as a surveillance camera, though far better than ours). This aspect of Islamic faith almost completely removes the need for legal monitoring for the members of society are not only dedicated voluntary participants, they are also self-monitored. Thus, while the spiritual elevation of individual human life introduces self-monitoring of individuals' own behavior following the universal moral code of conduct, physical and mental development facilitates unimpeded material progress leading to the growth of civilization.

There are two important benefits that are derived from this process. First, self-monitoring eliminates, or at least, reduces the need for instituting an elaborate and complex legal system along with its very expensive monitoring system; second, it motivates every member of society to participate voluntarily in personal and community development. While the first frees huge amounts of society's resources – both human and material – for utilization in developmental activities, the second leads to economic development or more appropriately, human development. The latter aspect eliminates the social conflicts and tensions caused by the dissatisfaction stemming from extreme inequity and poverty endemic in contemporary systems. This again minimizes the amount of resources needed for conflict resolution and the administration of justice in the systems devoid of any role for the spiritual aspect of human living. The resources saved can be used for human development.

RELEVANCE OF ECONOMIC DEVELOPMENT

Economists have for a long time used the concepts of "economic growth" and "economic development" interchangeably. It was only in the late

1960s that they began to distinguish between them,[1] unfortunately only to return in the 1980s to emphasizing the importance of economic growth for prosperity and applying the policy of growth the world over. The only remnant of the recognition remains in the form of the human development index constructed and published annually by the United Nations Development Program.[2] Islam, however, recognized the importance of economic development for human development and applied the policy and achieved extraordinary results in the seventh century AC.

At this point, the meanings of growth and development need to be explained. Economic growth refers to the increase in per capita income accompanied by improvements in technology and changes in the structure of the economy from primary to manufacturing and technology-based production. In contrast, economic development means creating an environment for the realization of human personality to its maximum potential for every individual in society. Thus, economic development implies affording the members of society the opportunity to realize their human development to their fullest potential. In essence, development includes growth and adds a human content to it. Growth measures economic progress as the increase in societal income (wealth) without considering who is enjoying this wealth. On the other hand, development takes into account the implications of rising wealth for the general population concerning food security, nutritional standards, healthcare, longevity, education, etc.

Achieving economic prosperity by the state mandate under communism and by the allocation of most of the resources to a small business class under capitalism is a policy of economic growth. It is a fast way to attaining economic prosperity and technological progress. However, it takes place at a huge cost to humanity in the form of poverty, hunger, malnutrition, homelessness, unemployment, lack of medical care, lack of education, etc. The extreme inequity generated causes dissatisfaction and a lack of respect for the law, resulting in the incarceration of a large number of people. Furthermore, it is not only costly to society in lost productivity owing to workers' dissatisfaction and increased expenditure in the administration of the law, but also makes the system inherently unstable. The contributions by the system to civilization therefore face the constant threat of being lost. The disintegration of the erstwhile USSR illustrates the consequences of this instability.

The Islamic policy of economic development internalizes the policy of human development along with increasing societal wealth. This simply means that every member of society is afforded the opportunity to participate in the generation of wealth and to share equitably in the prosperity gained. Thus, economic development establishes a just and equitable system. Under this system, the economic prosperity and technological progress achieved are steady and their contributions to civilization are stable and less likely to be lost as a result of inherent forces of destruction.

This type of economic and human development is based on the Islamic policy of ensuring the dedicated voluntary participation of all by winning their hearts and minds. The just and equitable basis of prosperity produces steady and stable contributions to civilization, which are more or less permanent, unless external forces threaten to destroy them.

ISLAMIC ECONOMIC SYSTEM

An economic system is distinguished by the type of ownership and use of property, the nature of the exchange mechanism, the method of allocation of resources and distribution of income and wealth, and the role of society in modifying the outcomes. The contrast between the capitalist and the communist systems is clear and well known. The features of the Islamic system, however, need a detailed description, for the system is new to the modern world and it overlaps both capitalism and communism.

The ownership of property is a critical factor determining the nature of a system and needs to be addressed first. In Islam, God has created everything in the universe and therefore, God owns everything, including humans. The humans, as vicegerents of God on earth, are given the trusteeship of everything else – the right to use and preserve everything else for their welfare. This right to use, however, comes with duties and responsibilities. Unlike both capitalism and communism, Islam grants humans the right to use, not the right to own. The substantive difference being that the right to own grants the right to use in any way that the owner wishes, whereas the right to use puts restrictions and obligations defined by the owner. God, in Islam, has imposed elaborate restrictions on the use of resources and attached important obligations to that right. Islam, thus, introduces moderation into this important institution of private property and frees the society and its members from the tyranny of ownership of resources by either private individuals or the state. This right to use in

Islam, however, is granted to private individuals as in capitalism, not to the collective authority of the society as in communism. Society, however, is given the responsibility of insuring that the individual members discharge their duties and fulfill their obligations in using the resources. Therefore, although Islam grants individuals the right to use resources, it also insures their appropriate utilization by imposing duties and responsibilities on this right, and entrusts society with the authority to enforce them. Islam is thus a moderate blend of an individual's right to freedom, and the social authority's duty to regulate it, that is, a blend of capitalism and socialism.

Given the private right to use resources, the Islamic system functions by the operation of the market. Free private enterprise is at the heart of an Islamic economy, for it encourages initiative and drive, facilitates innovations, and rewards productivity. God declares in the Qur'an, "He it is Who created for you all that is in the earth" (2:29). The Qur'an enjoins, "When the prayer is ended, disperse in the land and seek of God's bounty" (62:10). These verses categorically suggest that the earth is for humans to explore and utilize. The Qur'an further says, "God has made subservient to you whatever is in the heavens and whatever is in the earth and granted you His bounties both manifest and hidden" (31:20). These verses ascertain the place of material well-being in Muslim life. In fact, Islam sets no limit on how much an individual can earn and spend; rather, it sets firm restrictions on how an individual earns and spends his/her income. The permissible and forbidden methods and activities of earning and spending are clearly stated. The Qur'an declares, "Allah has glorified trade and forbidden *Ribā*." (2:275). *Ribā* is a predetermined fixed return on loans, irrespective of whether the borrower makes a profit or a loss. This statement implies that although Islam encourages the productive circulation of income and wealth, it clearly forbids the unproductive accumulation of wealth and exploitative earning of incomes. Hoarding for the purpose of raising prices and gambling are examples of these forbidden activities.

Islam requires self-reliance on the part of every member of the society and discourages dependence on others. Two stories from the life of Prophet Muhammad convincingly illustrate the point. One day a man came to the Prophet for help. The Prophet, instead of giving him a handout, asked him if he had anything at home that he could spare. When the man told him that he had a few kitchen pots that could be spared, he asked him to bring them to him. After the man brought the pots, the Prophet auctioned them to his Companions, gave some of the money from the sale to the man to buy food for himself and his family, and gave the remaining amount to him to buy an axe for cutting wood from the forest.

On another occasion, the Prophet noticed that a man was staying in the mosque, praying for days and going out only for the calls of nature. He also noticed that another man had been bringing him food everyday. So the Prophet called on the man and asked him why he was staying in the mosque all the time, the name of the man who was bringing him food, if he had a family and children, and who was taking care of them. The man replied that he wanted to worship God all the time, the man was his brother, he had a family and children, and his brother was taking care of them. After hearing all this, the Prophet said, "Your brother is a better worshipper than you are."

These two stories clearly suggest that dependence on others is not an acceptable way of living in Islam for people of ability. Self-reliance is admirable and therefore encouraged. Prophet Muhammad said, "Nobody has ever eaten a better meal than that which he has earned by working with his own hand."[3] The Prophet is also reported to have said, "If God provides anyone of you with an opportunity for earning a livelihood, let him not leave it unexploited until it is exhausted or becomes disagreeable to him."[4] These sayings clearly indicate the importance of economic prosperity in Muslim life. More importantly, the concept of worshiping God in Islam is broad and far-reaching guiding human behavior in this respect: living life on earth by following the commandments of God is a better way of worshiping Him. This insures participation by everyone in income generation and offers them the opportunity to explore their potential, and to make the best possible contribution to society.

In requiring self-reliance and participation in productive activities by every member of society, Islam insures that they enjoy an equal opportunity in acquiring complementary resources with which to work. The first and the most important complementary resource is human capital, that is, knowledge, and Islam makes the acquisition of this resource obligatory for every Muslim man and woman.[5] The importance of learning is also evident from the first injunction revealed by God to Prophet

Muhammad: "Read in the name of your Lord Who created. Created humans from a clot" (96:1–2). In addition to enjoining learning, God is also talking about the science of creation in this very first revelation. This strongly indicates that spiritual knowledge requires a proper understanding of the functioning of the material world. That this knowledge relates to material aspects of living is also evident from the Prophet's instruction, "If necessary, seek knowledge in China."[6] Islamic civilization is based on this role of learning in Muslim life, as is testified by the Muslim contributions to civilization as described elsewhere in this book.

In addition, Islam establishes important economic institutions to provide everyone in society with material resources so that nobody is deprived of the opportunity to participate productively. The institution of inheritance is one such institution. Unlike the Western institution of primogeniture, which grants sole ownership of the parent's estate to the first child only, Islam grants inheritance rights to a large number of the members of the family. The members who are entitled to a share in the estate and their respective shares are clearly defined and predetermined by Islam and nobody has any authority to change them. Even the holder of the estate, unlike the Western system of granting rights to the owner to give his/her estate to whoever he/she desires, does not have the authority or even the right to deprive any member of his/her share by way of writing a will before death.

These injunctions and institutions, in addition to providing complementary resources to almost every member of society for productive participation, eliminate the potential for the concentration of income and wealth, on the one hand, and creation of poverty, on the other. The distribution of the estate among a large number of inheritors after the death of a relative attacks these problems at the root and reduces the potential for the creation of poverty. In addition, it reduces the chances of inefficient utilization of assets by large asset-holders, who might simply rely on unearned income, and it increases the productive efficiency of assets by innovative inheritors. Note that the larger the number of people receiving complementary resources, the greater is the probability of inventions and innovations in the system. Islam, thus, engages the largest possible number of people in production and thereby encourages efficiency, induces inventions and innovations, and facilitates economic prosperity. Most of all, this prosperity is achieved in a just and equitable process by the increased circulation of productive resources in the system.

Islam, however, recognizes that there will always be some less fortunate people in society, such as those suffering from physical and mental disabilities, victims of natural calamities, the socially displaced, and the demographically and economically handicapped, such as orphans, widows, the elderly, the unemployed, etc. Here Islam deals with the problem at both individual and social levels to insure that, according to the Qur'an, "wealth does not circulate only among your rich" (59:7).

At the individual level, Islam requires the more fortunate to take care of the less fortunate in society. Prophet Muhammad said, "He is not a true Muslim who takes his fill and his neighbor goes to bed hungry."[7] This, however, is not prescribed as showing pity for the less fortunate, but as a way of expressing gratitude to God for making them more fortunate. As vicegerents of God on earth, every individual, including the less fortunate, has been granted a minimum of human dignity by Him. Therefore, this means of giving charity must also be dignified. In essence, God has granted the needy a legitimate share in the wealth of the rich. In this sense, the rich simply perform their obligation to (worship) God by giving a share of their wealth to the needy. Zakah, one of the five pillars of Islam, is one such obligation required of a Muslim. After some deductions, 2.5 percent of accumulated wealth is to be paid as a welfare tax at the end of the year. Although as a proportion of the total accumulated wealth this seems insignificant, I will show that this is a very potent economic instrument in eradicating poverty completely from society with the least impact on the holder of wealth.

Islam actually makes it a social responsibility for the community to eradicate poverty. The existence of poverty in society is considered to be an abominable sin for the community as a whole. The most serious sin in Islam is *kufr*, which means denying the Authority of God. Prophet Muhammad said, "Poverty is a sin worse than *kufr*."[8] This implies that poverty is not tolerated in an Islamic system, or more categorically, a system that tolerates poverty denies the Authority of God, and therefore, is not an Islamic system.

In conclusion this section can be summarized by saying that the Islamic economic system combines the beneficial characteristics of both capitalism and communism, yet is free of their undesirable features. The application of free enterprise and market mechanisms along with the use of egalitarian principles ensures the system is both efficient and equitable. The absence of ownership rights over resources and of unrestricted authority for their use by both the individual and the state frees society from the tyranny of ownership and use. In this sense, the Islamic system is a balanced middle path – a moderate system devised for the benefit of humanity.

POVERTY AND DISTRIBUTION INEQUITY IN THE USA

To illustrate the effectiveness of these simple and straightforward principles of Islam in dealing with the problems of a complex modern economy, the absolute poverty and inequity in the distribution of income and wealth in the United States of America are a useful example. The United States is the most affluent country in the world today and has the most technologically advanced economy. However, the country suffers from a serious problem of chronic absolute poverty – hunger, homelessness, and lack of medical care, in spite of the fact that it has all the means at its disposal to eliminate this blight from its society. At the same time, it has a very high level of inequity in the distribution of income and wealth, which is becoming worse with time.

Absolute poverty is defined as the inability of a family to afford the minimum basic needs of life and therefore, a condition of living below the standard of subsistence. In the United States, an official poverty line is constructed based on this definition and all those falling below this line are defined as absolute poor. This poverty line is calculated as the cost of the least expensive bundle of vegetarian diet providing the minimum nutritional needs, multiplied by a factor of three to include the cost of the other basic needs of life – shelter, clothing, medical care, etc. The poverty line income used by the US government in 1999 was $8,501 for a single individual, $10,869 for a family of two, $13,290 for a family of three, and $17,029 for a family of four.[9] Based on these thresholds, the estimate shows that 32.4 million people or 11.8 percent of the total US population were in absolute poverty in 1999.[10]

The 1999 census figures also show that 42.6 million people, that is, over 15.5 percent of the total population do not have any form of medical coverage.[11] The Urban Institute (2000)[12] reported over two million homeless people in 1996. This figure continued to rise, and increased by 15 percent in 2000 over that of 1999, according to the Conference of Mayors.[13] The Tufts University Center on Hunger, Poverty, and Nutrition Policy[14] estimates that 12 million people are chronically hungry, while more than 35 million suffer food insecurity (1997 figures). Note that families which are marginally above the poverty line can fall below the line at any time – hence they are also food insecure along with the poor. A US Department of Agriculture Report[15] shows that one in every ten US households suffers food insecurity.

This condition of poverty has serious adverse effects on human development. Lack of proper nutrition and medical care causes physical and mental debilitya, stunted growth in children, susceptibility to diseases, and ultimately, premature death. These effects are apparent in the human development index constructed by the United Nations Development Program. The United States has the highest infant and maternal mortality rate and lowest longevity for both males and females in the industrial world, although it has the highest per capita GDP adjusted for purchasing power parity. [16]

Why does the United States have such high levels of poverty and hunger problem? A look at the minimum wage figures can provide an insight into this situation. Assume that the minimum wage is $5.65 per hour and that an individual works full time, that is, 40 hours per week and 50 weeks per year. The weekly earning will be $226, assuming that $26 will be deducted for social security, temporary disability, etc. the weekly take-home pay is $200. This gives an annual income of $10,000, which is less than the poverty level income for a family of two. Assume again that a one-bedroom apartment costs $500 a month that will take away $6,000 from the yearly income, leaving only $4,000 for everything else. If food costs $300 a month, a total of $3,600 per year, only $400 is left for the whole year for transportation, clothing, medical care, education, electricity, gas, phone, etc. – an impossible task. Poverty is the inevitable outcome.

How the low wage perpetuates the condition of poverty is clear from the trend in minimum wage over time. The US Department of Labor compiled a list of minimum wage figures for a long period of time.[17] This list shows that the real minimum wage in 1998 dollars, instead of going up, has actually gone down over the years. In 1968, the minimum wage was $7.49 (in 1998 $). It fell to $6.19 in 1977, $4.40 in 1989, and rose

slightly to $5.23 in 1997, but is still far below the 1968 figure. This is
exactly the reason why hunger has been continually increasing over time.
Research by Tufts University Center for Hunger, Poverty, and Nutrition
Policy, shows that there were 20 million hungry Americans in 1985,
which increased to 30 million in 1992, and 35 million in 1997.

One important aspect of the US economy's health needs to be highlighted here. The problem of poverty and hunger just described prevailed
during a period of unprecedented economic prosperity – during the
1990s. The economy was growing steadily at about 4 percent annually
with almost no unemployment, zero inflation, and very low interest rates.

Table 7.1: *Households' Share of Income and Wealth in the USA (1989) (percent)*

	Top 20%	Top 1%	Top 5%	Bottom 20%	Bottom 80%	Bottom 95%
Income	55.5	16.4	29.7	3.1	44.5	70.3
Wealth	84.6	40.9	62.8%	-1.4	15.4	37.2
Financial Wealth	93.9	48.1	72.2	-2.3	6.1	27.8

Source: Wolff, *Economics of Poverty.*

Who, then, is enjoying this economic prosperity? The figures in Table
7.1 give a clear answer to this question. These figures relate to 1989, the
latest analysis done by Wolff.[18] The top 20 percent of US households
enjoy 55.5 percent of the national income, a share greater than that of the
bottom 80 percent of households, whereas the bottom 20 percent enjoy a
meager 3.1 percent. The distribution of net wealth (assets minus debts) is
even worse, the richest 20 percent receiving 84.6 percent (leaving 15.4
percent for the bottom 80 percent of households), whereas the bottom 95
percent receive only 37.2 percent. The shares of the top 1 and 5 percent
are 40.9 and 62.8 percent, respectively. Worst is the distribution of financial wealth (financial assets minus financial liabilities), with 93.9 percent
going to the richest 20 percent and 27.8 percent to the bottom 95 percent.
Here the shares of the top 1 and 5 percent of the households are respectively, 48.1 and 72.2 percent.

Studies also show that this inequity in the distribution of income and wealth increased further during the 1990s.[19] While the real wage has been decreasing, CEO pay has been skyrocketing – the average yearly CEO pay reached $5.6 million in 1996, raising the CEO workers pay ratio to 209:1 from 44:1 in the 1960s. In addition, the tax burden has shifted continually from the rich to the middle class during the 1980s and 1990s.[20]

ISLAMIC SOLUTION TO POVERTY AND INEQUALITY IN THE UNITED STATES

The most important thrust of the Islamic system is the development of the human personality. Once that has been achieved and put in place, the rest becomes easy, for the injunctions of the permissible and the forbidden are obeyed. The implementation of a policy thus becomes a matter of informing the community about the policy and it is carried out by dedicated and self-monitored members of society.

In the absence of such a system, however, the implementation of an Islamic policy in the United States would have to depend on the existing system of external monitoring. Since personal material well-being is the only consideration in this materialistic secular society, the policy has a greater chance of success if it entails a smaller personal sacrifice than that already in existence. Therefore, I will give a brief description of the Islamic instruments for reducing poverty and inequity, though they might not be easy to use outside a fully-fledged Islamic system. I will then make a strong case for the introduction of the system of Zakah to solve the problems, for it requires a much smaller personal sacrifice and is easy to implement.

The introduction of the Islamic law of inheritance can go a long way in reducing inequity and poverty. Similarly, the application of the laws governing permissible and forbidden activities and the methods of earning and spending wealth can eliminate many sources of the accumulation and concentration of income and wealth and the concomitant generation of poverty. Gambling, the production, trade, and consumption of drugs, hoarding, and speculative manipulation of the market are examples of such activities. It is the consumers' behavior that determines what the market supplies and thereby provides the incentive for these activities. Islam places great emphasis on the consumption behavior of an individual as an economic entity. Correcting individual behavior with respect to the demand for drugs, for example, could eliminate the problem of drug production and drug dealing. The United States might never have to fight drug wars in other countries and spend huge amounts of resources that could be easily used for fighting poverty at home.

More importantly, the United States will not have to spend huge amount of resources in fighting the drug war at home and in filling its adult correctional institutions with inmates. This will turn millions of American youth into productive resources, which, by itself will reduce poverty markedly, for the families and children of the incarcerated individuals are sentenced to poverty by their incarceration.

All these, however, require Islamic education and the development of Islamic personalities. In their absence, the Islamic institution of charity – both voluntary and obligatory – can play an effective role in eliminating poverty completely and thereby diminishing inequity to a certain extent. The United States already has a tradition of supporting the poor with the welfare system and people make generous voluntary donations. The problem is that the system is designed to support the poor, not to bring them out of poverty, thereby having the undesirable effect of perpetuating the problem. The introduction of Zakah could not only eliminate poverty, but also convert the poor into productive members of society. Moreover, the required payment is so small a percentage of the asset-holders' accumulations that it is not expected to have any adverse effect on the incentive to the productive accumulation and utilization of assets. This measure, coupled with the productive participation of the erstwhile poor, could lead to equitable prosperity, rather than stifling growth, which, it is asserted, can happen with conventional redistribution policies.

The zakah, translated as a welfare tax, is an obligatory wealth tax imposed and collected by society to help the less fortunate and to convert those among them who are physically and mentally able into productive members of society. It is only 2.5 percent of the assets accumulated at the end of the year after some deductions, such as the value of owner-occupied homes and of a small amount of jewelry regularly worn by women. The early Islamic society established by Prophet Muhammad practiced this instrument with great success. Indeed, within a few years of its institution, it was so successful that the system could not find anybody deserving of support. It is worth mentioning that the early Islamic economy was not at all affluent compared with the US economy today.

To see what could happen if the instrument of Zakah were institutionalized, I will quote the figures estimated by Wilhelm[21] and used by Ackerman and Alstott[22] in their proposal for a wealth tax to replace the income tax. Using a household exemption of $80,000, they show that a 2 percent wealth tax could yield the revenue of $378 billion per year. Adjusting this figure for 2.5 percent zakah rate, total yearly zakah collection could be $472.5 billion. Now, by dividing this amount among the 32.4 million poor, American society could pay $14,583 per year to every individual, which is $43,750 for a family of three. This calculation shows that society can eliminate poverty completely in just one year. This measure would give the families not just the support, but also enough to invest in educa-tion, attain occupational skills, and become productive. In a few years of its implementation, this social help might fully eliminate the need for any external support for these families.

To compare this zakah figure with the welfare expenditure in the country, take the two important programs mainly geared towards the poor: Aid to Families with Children and Food Stamps. Both federal and state governments spent in 1996 a little over $40 billion on these pro-grams, which is expected to be even smaller now as a result of the work-fare reform. In any case, this expenditure is only a small fraction of the total zakah money collection, underlining the important role zakah can play.

This zakah program, in addition to eliminating poverty, would reduce the problem of inequity also. The importance of this measure cannot be ignored, because it would reduce inequity from the bottom up, rather than the conventional method of top down. It is the top down method to which the wealthy in society object and resist; the bottom up method is welcomed and facilitated by everybody in society.

One more point needs mentioning here. The country spends $70 billion a year to keep about two million incarcerated behind bars. The elimination of poverty by the institution of zakah most probably will reduce the level of incarceration and save resources for productive utili-zation. This suggests that the zakah program could go a long way not only in solving poverty, but also other problems from which society suffers.

CONCLUSIONS

I would like to conclude this chapter by emphasizing that the Islamic economic system is not only feasible in a modern economy, but indeed is also the answer to its problems. The modern system has become complex and is growing more complex so as to make the issues intractable only because it denies one very important aspect of human life – the soul (spirit). It directs the whole system toward a fierce competition for gaining as many material possessions and as much power as possible. In the Darwinian battle for survival of the fittest, more appropriately, the battle for accession to position of wealth and power for the fittest, in the absence of any kind of moral code of behavior, secular modern society creates many problems with which it is absolutely ill-equipped to deal. The only thing it does is to enact more and more laws with stringent punishment for violation, but to no avail, for the allure of material possessions and power is much too great to keep the aspirants to material success from violating the law.

The Islamic system is simple and straightforward enough for everybody to understand, and its spiritual guidance is persuasive enough to make humanity abide by divine injunctions that are universally beneficial for humanity. In addition, society is geared towards creating and maintaining the environment for both the material and spiritual elevation of everyone in society. If applied, this system could successfully eliminate the problems of the complex modern economy in simple and straightforward ways and could lead to economic development, rather than growth. The institution of zakah illustrates this possibility clearly and well.

8

Islamic Financial Institutions in the United States: Viability and Prospects

ABDEL-HAMEED M. BASHIR

ABSTRACT

Since the prescriptions of Islam prohibit charging or receiving interest, Muslims in the West, particularly those in the United States, find themselves effectively unable to deal with the interest-based financial institutions. Hence, a genuine need arises for establishing financial institutions that serve a growing Muslim population while at the same time adhering to the rules and regulations of the US financial system. The question now is: How can the Islamic financial institutions bridge the gap between religious constraints and financial regulations?

INTRODUCTION

THERE IS CONSENSUS among Muslim jurists and scholars that the interest rate charged by conventional banks is the prohibited *ribā*. While Muslims adhere closely to the directives of the Qur'an and Sunnah, it is sometimes helpful to understand the rationale for these prohibitions. It has been argued by many prominent Western economists that the system based on interest and debt is unstable and subject to financial crises. The 1990s witnessed many debt crises in different parts of the world, including Latin America, East Asia and Russia. The single most common factor of all these crises was bank loans made at excessively high rates of interest. When the indebted companies and currency traders defaulted, the whole financial systems tumbled. The Islamic financial system, based on participation and risk-sharing offers a viable remedy for the world debt crisis. Under the Islamic modes of financing, the lender is expected to share part of the risk of the investment. Accordingly, Islamic financing encourages active participation and asserts that money borrowed is not entitled to a reward. Thus the system of shared risk is expected to reduce the possibility of financial crises and to be more fair and equitable. Hence, Muslims are encouraged to abide by the tenets of Islam and not deal with interest because of the great torment that awaits those who ignore this Islamic injunction. Therefore, it is imperative that Muslims in the West in general, and in the United States in particular, establish financial institutions that provide them with interest-free choices.

Recently, a survey by the Council on American Islamic Relations (CAIR) and other Muslim organizations, estimated the number of Muslims in the United States and Canada to be over 10 million. The survey went further to conclude that sizeable portions of the Muslim community are middle class professionals with a major savings pool.[1] One major lesson to be learned from this recent study is that the Muslim communities in the West are dynamic and changing over time. During the 1960s and 1970s, the pioneering Muslim emigrants (mainly students) were occupied with organizing themselves on college campuses to preserve their Islamic identity. During the 1980s and 1990s, the process had changed to building local institutions like mosques, schools, and Islamic centers, as well as social, cultural, and professional organizations. Certainly, the urgent challenge facing the Muslims in the twenty-first century is building economic and political bases for empowerment and active participation. In particular, Muslims are faced with urgent needs for financial institutions that conform to the tenets of Islam. The absence of Islamically-oriented institutions has forced Muslims to deal with the interest-based conventional system. Notwithstanding the religious and secular constraints arising when dealing with *ribā*-based institutions, Muslim communities found themselves financially weak and marginalized. Being relatively small communities, large financial institutions were uninterested in serving their needs or catering for their religious restrictions. Consequently, the two groups mostly affected by this situation were Muslim consumers and small businesses for, historically, these two groups relied heavily on local banks for their credit and payments needs.

It is imperative that small businesses are supported, because they play an essential role in the economic prosperity of smaller communities. Hence, for all practical purposes, there exists an indisputable demand for financial institutions providing services and products to satisfy the needs of the Muslim clientele. The question is: Why is the development of Islamic financial institutions in the United States so slow or limited? The purpose of this chapter is to shed some light on the factors limiting the growth of Islamic financial institutions within the US financial system. The second section of the chapter focuses on the constraints facing these institutions and how to overcome them. The third section discusses the current state of the existing institutions, their challenges and potential successes, while the fourth section highlights new opportunities and unsatisfied needs. Some concluding remarks are given in the last section.

OBSTACLES AND CHALLENGES

Theoretically, Islamic financial institutions have to overcome many obstacles before they can operate in the US financial system. It is important to keep in mind that some of these obstacles have become less restrictive recently. Islamic institutions have a better chance to succeed, given the profound changes just taking place in the US banking industry; the most obvious being mergers, deregulation, information technology, and financial integration. The implications of these changes for the profitability and safety of banks have been widely discussed. Meanwhile, the implications of these changes for Islamic financial institutions are yet to be examined. One may legitimately argue that the current changes will benefit Islamic finance by relaxing the entry restrictions to the financial markets. If Islamic banks are allowed to operate in the United States, (as community banks or national banks), the Muslim communities will have access to financial services that are compatible with the Shariʿah. Surely, regulations such as the Community Reinvestment Act (CRA), which requires banks to lend in all areas in which they take deposits, would certainly benefit Islamic consumers and small businesses.[2] On the contrary, one might argue that the new changes would not be helpful to Islamic financial institutions for two reasons. First, Islamic financial institutions cannot succeed in a *ribā*-based environment because they have to adhere to regulations. Second, because of their size, Islamic institutions will not be able to compete with large organizations created by mergers. None the less, for Islamic financial institutions to be able to succeed in the United States, they have to overcome certain impediments. These include regulation, innovation, competition, lack of accounting standards, and the perception of the Muslim communities.

FINANCIAL REGULATIONS

Until recently, the primary constraint hindering the growth and development of Islamic banks in the US financial markets is financial regulation. If Islamic banks, for example, were chartered to operate in the United States, they would be required to adhere to the same set of rules and regulations applied to their counterparts, regardless of the nature and scope of their operations.[3] The Banking Act of 1933, which requires the separation of the banking and securities industries, was a major obstacle to operating a bank on an Islamic basis.[4] However, until now, Islamic banks were not able to apply for a charter in the United States, because the Islamic modes of contract (*Muḍarabah*) put the depositors' funds at risk, contrary to the safety measures demanded by regulators. Accordingly, the rapid growth (15 percent annually) and the global success of Islamic banks worldwide have led many traditional banks to open windows for Islamic deposits (Citibank). Another major obstacle to the operation of Islamic banks in the US financial system is the reserves requirement. The equity-like nature of Islamic profit-loss sharing (PLS) deposits makes them different than ordinary deposits in a conventional bank. Many jurists and Islamic economists argue against subjecting PLS deposits to reserve requirements. They argue that since PLS deposits are neither guaranteed nor entitled to fixed returns, subjecting them to reserve requirements will be an extra burden on both the depositor and the institution, since reserve requirements provide no returns.[5] Furthermore, deposit insurance (and insurance in general) could also be considered a barrier, given the controversy over the conventional insurance contract. However, the passage of Grann-Leach-Bliley Financial Services Modernization Act of 1999 (GLBA) has made establishing of an Islamic bank in the United States possible and imminent.[6] In particular, Islamic banks would have to pay more attention to their Camel rating (acronym based on five areas: capital adequacy, assets quality, management, earnings, and liquidity) in order to adhere to the US financial regulations.

FINANCIAL PRODUCTIONS

Another obstacle hampering the expansion of Islamic financial institutions in the United States is the financial instruments available for mobilizing and utilizing Muslims' savings. The current instruments can be classified under two headings: equity-like and mark-up and debt-like instruments. In fact, there are many types of instruments (contracts) in each category, whereby jurists and financial practitioners have established their validity and conformity with the Shariʿah. None the less, the existing instruments are limited in scope and can hardly cope with the contemporary financial needs. Many Muslims and non-Muslims lack a clear understanding of their applicability to this continually innovative financial environment. Hence, Islamic financial institutions have to develop and innovate (financial engineering) short-term financial instruments that satisfy the Shariʿah requirement while at the same time allowing banks to diversify their portfolios and secure short-term funds if needed. Islamic financial institutions also have to invest heavily in familiarizing their potential customers and clients with these instruments before they can expect to attract new customers or survive the competition.

ACCOUNTING STANDARDS

Another constraint that could be detrimental for the growth and development of Islamic financial institutions in the US markets is the lack of standard accounting principles that facilitate disclosure and surveillance of bank performance. Standardization of accounting policies is just as important for Islamic financial institutions as it is for conventional ones, and for the same reason: to facilitate meaningful comparisons and analyses of results. In most cases, it is not possible to use the conventional accounting principles and apply them to the Islamic financial concepts because the frameworks of the two systems are different. Recently, the Accounting and Auditing Organization for Islamic Financial Institutions (AAOIFI) has introduced twelve (12) accounting standards, which precisely cover disclosures and the transparency of the balance sheets and financial statements. It is hoped that, by adopting the AAOIFI standards, the nature of Islamic financial institutions business activities becomes more transparent.

COMPETITION

For Islamic financial institutions to survive in the US financial system, they should be innovative and have sufficient capital. More importantly, the ability of Islamic institutions to exist in a well-developed and highly innovative system depends on whether they can compete with well-established, well-capitalized institutions. In an environment of financial integration, where the securities and insurance companies have recently been allowed to enter the banking business, Islamic financial institutions will face tough competition in both the deposit and financial service markets. Therefore, Islamic financial institutions should be innovative and aggressive in designing new modes of financing in order to attract deposits and provide financial services for their customers.

On the other hand, financial integration would enable Islamic financial institutions to reduce costs and diversify their portfolios to generate more profits and provide competitive returns. The fact that Islamic banks do not guarantee the nominal values of their deposits and do not provide fixed returns creates a strong incentive for risk taking. Hence, it would be necessary to raise the capital ratio to reduce additional hazards. In particular, enough capital is needed to reduce the risk of insolvency (capital ratio more than 8 percent). In a well-regulated financial system, competition is necessary for efficiency and quality. A certain level of competition is required before these institutions can meet the demands of a growing Muslim population.

COMMITMENT

For Islamic financial institutions to flourish and expand, we need authentic presence and commitment. Authentic presence requires commitment to the Shariʿah from both the institutions and their clientele. More importantly, the Muslim community's awareness of these institutions and its willingness to patronize them are key ingredients for success. An Islamic bank cannot succeed without clients who are committed to the notion of Islamic financing. Equally, the Islamically committed customers cannot patronize a financial institution unless the institution satisfies their religious and financial needs, that is, unless the institution provides services similar to the un-Islamic alternatives available in the market while satisfying the tenets of the Shariʿah. On the other hand, being socially responsible, Islamic financial institutions should operate as community banks, mobilizing the savings of the community and reinvesting it in the same community. An Islamic financial institution can effectively and efficiently play a social and religious role by pooling the zakah money and redistributing it in the community. However, these institutions cannot succeed unless they become committed to their mission, abide by the Shariʿah, and provide for the financial needs of their customers. Indeed, the mosque, and other social and educational institutions can play a pivotal role in educating the community about the importance of patronizing the Islamic financial institutions.

THE STATE OF THE EXISTING ISLAMIC FINANCIAL INSTITUTIONS

Certainly, the enormous bloc of Muslims in the United States cannot be overlooked in the growth and prosperity of the US economy. The phenomenal surge or fall in the US market (as indicated by various indices like DJIA, NASDAQ, S&P500) in the 1990s has inspired many people, Muslims included, to invest in stocks and other financial assets. Consequently, few institutions have emerged to mobilize Muslim resources and provide them with a bridge to economic and financial security. The bulk of the Islamic institutions operating in the US financial markets today focus on assets management, consumer financing, and non-bank activities. Apparently, the success of some of these institutions has inspired companies like the Dow Jones, International Investor, and the FTSE International to launch global Islamic Index series (DJII, TII Global Islamic Index, and FTSE International) to track the performance of investing in Islamic equity funds. Despite being small and fragmented, some of the existing institutions have made major successes in the areas on which they concentrate. In many cases the annual returns have outperformed both large and small capitalizing stocks in the last few years. For example for Amana Income Fund, the average annual return for the last 10 years was 11.69 percent compared with S&P500's return of 17.43 percent, while Amana Growth Fund averaged 17.81 percent compared with Russell 2000's 10.53 percent for the same period. Between 1996 and 1999, the Dow Jones Islamic Index Fund averaged 27.25 percent, outperforming S&P 500 (24.37 percent) and Russell 2000 (12.86 percent). Furthermore, the NAIT annual returns have averaged 6 percent compared with 5.6 percent deposit rates.

CHALLENGES AHEAD

The absence of interest-free banks from the US financial landscape can be attributed to the American regulations, as stated earlier, or to simple economics. Whatever the reason, the apparent success of existing Islamic funds has attracted many traditional institutions to consider providing Islamic financing (Citibank, Fannie Mae). Realizing the importance of satisfying the religious needs of the Muslim community, the Office of the Comptroller of the Currency (OCC) is reviewing several applications for a charter by Islamic financial institutions. Moreover, the wide use of the Internet has made it possible for foreign banks to provide their services to Muslims in the United States. Online Islamic banking could benefit consumers by lowering fees or increasing returns on profit–loss deposits.

As we mentioned above, the existing institutions have concentrated their businesses on mutual savings (NAIT), real estate financing (UBK/Al-MANZIL, ISLAMIC CO-OP, MSI), car leasing and home financing (LARIBA), mutual funds and assets management (AMANA, DOW JONES ISLAMIC INDEX FUND, ISLAMIQ.COM), and insurance (TAKAAFUL USA). Obviously, the Muslim financial needs are not limited to what is provided by the existing Islamic institutions. One way to describe the problem is to think of Islamic consumers and small businesses. As consumers, people on fixed incomes cannot invest in stocks, which are the focus of these institutions, because of the high risk associated with them. There is, therefore, an urgent need for institutions specializing in Islamically viable low-risk investments to attract the savings of these groups (an Islamic pension fund?). Muslim students are also not well served by the existing institutions. Institutions specialising in student loans are undoubtedly needed to cater for this group. Institutionalizing zakah and *waqf* could be a viable solution to this problem. Muslim communities also need small business for *ḥalāl* products (stores), professional and specialized services, schools, etc. Because of their vital importance to the communities, these small businesses need specialized funding opportunities. Lastly, but not least, Islamic institutions should establish national foundations that give grants for research and community development.

CONCLUSION

The transformation of the banking system, the change in regulations, and information technology can all benefit the Muslim communities in the United States by allowing Islamic financial institutions to operate under both the American regulations and the tenets of the Shariʿah. The success of the existing Islamic institutions has paved the way for new services, new instruments, and new institutions.

9

Where do We Go from Here? Muslim Contribution to Civilization: The Harbinger of the Third Renaissance

SYED ALI AHSANI

T HE 1992 QUINCENTENARY celebrations of Columbus's discovery of America in 1492 was a turning point in the Muslim intellectual revival set in motion following the Second World War. Outside Spain, the first international conference on Islamic Spain in al-Hamra, of which I was the Chief Coordinator, was held in Lahore in 1991. Over 60 Muslim scholars, including 23 from outside the Subcontinent, presented papers on the glorious contribution of Islamic Spain to civilization.

From 1150 AC to the sixteenth century, Jewish, Christian, and Muslim scholars from Western Europe and Spain translated books from Arabic into Latin in the Toledo Academy established by Alfonso, Sabio the Wise. The translations were then distributed to academic centers in Europe, where they became the basis of the Renaissance, the revival of knowledge in Europe.

Unfortunately, the proceedings of the Lahore Conference were not published. Included in the papers presented was a research article by Dr. Raisuddin Ahmed of Dacca University. He proved that Muslims first entered Spain during the time of ʿUthmān, the third Caliph, who commanded that they proceed to Istanbul overland. ʿUqbah ibn Nāfiʿ, the ruler of Egypt, and his brother entered Spain but had to return, for the Berbers accompanying him did not continue the expedition and further reinforcements were cut off. This was narrated by Dr. Mohammad

Hamidullah in his *Wathīqah al-Siyasiyyah*. Masumī has also written a paper on the same subject.

The Lahore Declaration adopted at the conference called for the establishment of chairs, courses on Islamic Spain, the naming of streets after illustrious scholars of the period, conferences and seminars, on Islamic Spain, and the translation and publication of pertinent manuscripts extant in Spain and elsewhere. However, it was left to the Association of Muslim Social Scientists (AMSS) to facilitate the accomplishment of some of these goals. They helped financially in organizing the first ever Regional Conference in Dallas on June 22–23, 2001, on Islamic Contributions to Civilization. Fourteen scholars from all over the United States, including the President of the International Institute of Islamic Thought (IIIT), presented well-researched works at the conference. Being well attended by scholars from all faiths communities, the event was a great success.

In the Dallas Declaration, it was agreed to establish a regional chapter of AMSS in the South-West of the United States, to hold a regional conference at least every two years, and to carry out other scholarly activities pertinent to the mission of the Association. A copy of the Press Release on the event was also issued.

The conference was publicized not only in the local media, but also in the regional, national, and international press. It was heartening to note that the message was echoed in California. Under the leadership of Imam Hamza Yusuf, a task force was created under Mr. Youssef Ismail to carry the message of Islamic contributions to civilization to US academia; and to establish mobile museums, subsequently leading to a fully-fledged museum on this theme. The Council of Humanities may also consider providing appropriate funds for the purpose. Detailed information material was supplied to the Coordinator. It was hoped that other AMSS chapters would also be established elsewhere, possibly in the West and the Mid-West, where Br Abdullah is keenly interested in this project.

Similar efforts are in the offing elsewhere in the United States and abroad. For instance, in Jacksonville, Mississippi, where a museum on Muslim Spain has been established, an exhibition on Muslim Spain was held from October 2001; and a documentary on Muslim Spain was prepared there. At Georgetown University, a Graduate Seminar was held in 1997 on the same theme. At South Methodist University, a museum on Spain has been established, displaying artifacts on its Muslim period. With publicity, similar on-going and proposed activities may come to light both in the United States and across the world. In Lahore, Pakistan, the al-Khawarizmi Science Society has shown great interest and published information on its website on the AMSS-SW regional conference. In Spain, an Islamic University has been founded, of which Dr. Ali Kettani is the Rector. In the United States, Salma Khadra Jayusi published two volumes in 1992 on the Muslim legacy in Spain. In Madrid itself, seminars were held during the 1992 month-long Quincentenary celebrations of Columbus's Discovery of America.

THE MISSION

In adopting Islamic Contributions to Civilization as an important topic a vital tool is utilized to generate true awareness of Islam and Muslims among neighbors, co-workers, and fellow compatriots. The benefits of doing so can be:

1. Following the event, an institutional framework would be created to promote inter-faith dialog, the exchange of ideas, communication, and methodology for establishing a genuine civil society in the United States.

2. Given the common Judeo-Christian-Islamic heritage, this endeavor would aim at making the United States a "Light unto Nations," as envisaged by William Jefferson, a moral superpower, based on the monotheistic concept of human rights, equality, justice, and mutual respect and peace both at home and in foreign relations.

3. On the model of the Toledo Academy, founded by Alfonso, the third king of the Jews, Christians, and Muslims, this institution-building would promote the Second Renaissance in the West, especially in the United States, on the foundations of common spirituality, family values, and shared knowledge and learning.

4. The broader Muslim community in the area would become aware of the contribution that their forebears made to human civilization.

5. The conference would project to teachers, corporations, and the political and social elite, the historical period of the flowering of knowledge in the Middle East (the so-called Dark Ages), heralding the Renaissance in Europe and the rise of the West to its present heights.

6. The publication of the proceedings would serve as a valuable source of research and instruction for students, and academic and non-academic scholars.

7. Following this event, the ground would be prepared for the establishment of a regional chapter of the Association of Muslim Social Scientists (AMSS) in the South and South Central Region, including Louisiana, which has a professional association of a substantial number of academicians as members.

8. A proposed quarterly journal, the *New Millennium Studies*, would be published by the AMSS-SW, which would be its regional vehicle, promoting research on the theme, apart from an electronic newsletter.

9. Following the tenth anniversary of the Conference on Islamic Spain, originally held in Lahore in 1991, this event would be repeated every two years, the first being an international conference in 2003.

10. Efforts would also be made to initiate courses on this topic in the universities of North Texas and elsewhere.

11. The event would also help in presenting a positive image, by removing the current unrealistic and negative stereotyping of Islam and Muslims in the media.

Knowledge is a continuum and the Muslim contribution to civilization is no exception. This contribution continued even after Islamic civilization had reached its pinnacle. Even during the period of its decline, Muslim scholars were busy writing books on various aspects of learning, both secular and religious.

How can another Renaissance be created? As is commonly understood, the European Renaissance took place from the fourteenth to the seventeenth century. Bearing in mind that it means the rebirth or revival of the humanistic flowering of knowledge in the arts and sciences, such a Renaissance first took place in the Middle Ages from the tenth to the fourteenth century, the era of glory for the Muslim civilization, mistakenly called the Dark Ages. As such, this will be the Third Renaissance, ushering in a Utopia and an era of peace, plenty, and prosperity. Let us hope that it will be achieved by the common endeavor of the Abrahamic faiths – Judaism, Christianity, and Islam.

Conceptually, the ground for revival has already been prepared with the principles laid down in the Qur'an and the Sunnah of the last Messenger. He is reported to have foretold that after the regime of dictatorship and authoritarian rule, *khilāfah* will follow. After thirty years of *khilāfah rāshidah*, monarchy and authoritarian rule were established in Muslim lands, which have continued to this day. Whether that system of government was sanctioned by the Qur'an and the Sunnah is another debate, on which ʿalims (religious scholars) hold differing views. Al-Māwardī considers that Muslim rulers may establish the Shariʿah but may be unjust. Ghazālī favors tolerance of an oppressive ruler to avoid total anarchy. Ibn Taymiyyah opines that a "*kāfir* [unbelieving] government which establishes justice is better than an oppressive Muslim regime." Ibn Ḥazm and some other scholars allow rebellion against an unjust and oppressive ruler. The essential point in this public discourse, whether relating to the political or any other field, is the fundamental question: What is the guiding principle of the Shariʿah?

Since the passing away of the Messenger, there was agreement among scholars that the Qur'an and the Sunnah and ijtihad and *Qiyās* (analogical reasoning or innovative thinking within the Islamic framework) formed the fundamental constitutive principles of the Shariʿah. The Messenger is reported to have asked Muʿadh ibn Jabal, who was about to be dispatched to govern Yemen, how he would decide matters. He expressed his satisfaction with Muʿadh's response that he would rely on the Qur'an, the Sunnah, and ijtihad. Later, Ijmaʿ or the consensus of the early Companions was added as the fourth principle of the Shariʿah.

However, Ibn Ḥazm, a great Shariʿah scholar of al-Andalus (d.1064) firmly rejected *Qiyās* and Ijmaʿ as *bidʿah* (prohibited innovation), thus confining the Shari'ah constitutive principles strictly to the Qur'an, the Sunnah, and ijtihad. He was opposed to *'Taqlīd'* (blind adherence). However, his advocacy of a *'Taqlīd'*, which harmonizes faith and reason was an idea later pronounced by Ibn Ṭufayl and Ibn Rushd (Averroes). Both Ibn Rushd and Ibn Ḥazm disavowed *'Qiyās'* (analogical reasoning), *'Ta'wīl'* (allegorical interpretation) for arriving at legal decisions. However, they all including Ghazālī agreed on reaching the truth, and were committed to the Qur'an and the Sunnah, and they disapproved of any overemphasis on natural phenomena to the neglect of Divine Revelation. They equally ridiculed the religious scholars for frowning upon natural sciences, and used logic as a tool for establishing proof. In addition, they agreed on the concept of knowledge.

Ibn Ḥazm's influence lasted for centuries. Despite adherence to the Ḥanbalite school, Ibn Taymiyyah (d.1328) was opposed to *Taqlīd* (imitation), relying on the Qur'an and the Sunnah, and favoring ijtihad (individual inquiry). Ibn Khaldūn followed Ibn Ḥazm on historiography, environmental determinism, and the conception of sciences in respect of vision, dream, alchemy, astrology, and music.

The ideas of Ibn Ḥazm influenced Europe in regard to the validity of the intellect for establishing proofs, arriving at the truth, advocacy of the harmony of faith and philosophy, and advocacy of a liberal arts education and interdependence and harmony of religious and secular sciences. His works were translated into Latin and other European languages, thus contributing to the flowering of European Renaissance.

How will the topic of Muslim contribution to civilization herald a new Renaissance? It can be achieved in the same way as was the Renaissance in Europe from the fourteenth to the seventeenth century, by the translation of works from the Eastern languages into the Western languages and wider dissemination, utilizing modern means including the Internet. Like the Toledo Academy (1150–1550 AC), many such academies, universities, and other educational institutions could be persuaded to allocate special research grants to Islam and its contribution to civilization with a view to holding conferences, publishing manuscripts, and conducting research into this topic.

To this end, the message of AMSS in the next thirty years has to be broad-based in building a consensus on a new research paradigm for arriving at the truth. The goal is to bridge the philosophical hiatus that currently divides the East and the West. This strategy of AMSS can and ought to be pursued as a movement, not merely relying on academic research in an ivory tower. A program of expansion of the AMSS mission by establishing its chapters as well as various discipline fora in various parts of the United States and abroad. In view of the current debate on the clash/dialog of civilizations, a special panel on the contributions of various cultures to world civilization, including those of Muslims, ought to be allocated to all AMSS national conventions to explore cultural interactions. Linkages ought to be established between AMSS and other professional organizations for collaborative projects on the theme.

EPILOGUE

THIS VOLUME has largely concentrated on Muslim contributions to specific fields of knowledge: basic and applied physical and biological sciences including medicine, legal and political theories and practices, economic and financial concepts, models, and institutions, etc. Here, we would like to shed some light on the general areas of emphasis in a societal order based on Islamic principles.

The conceptual foundations of such a superstructure governing human life and its pertinent inherent relationships, with the Creator, fellow humans, other living beings, as well as with its inanimate environment, lie in a set of such lasting universal principles that can tap, with basic freedoms, the optimal positive human potential for a sustained period. These principles, properly applied, can provide a new purpose in life and a sense of its right direction. They can also release in human beings their personal and collective creative genius, intellectual and spiritual vitality.[1]

Islam provided the world with modes of institutionalization, practical implementation of the sterling principles of monogenetic equality, human dignity, justice and fairness, and disciplined individual freedom. Above all, it provided the integrity of character based on an acute spiritual sense of accountability for one's deeds, and how best to treat one another, the fauna and flora, and the natural resources. These divine blessings are to be utilized for the benefit of the whole of humanity without frivolous wastefulness.

By implementing these principles, Muslims rebuilt the spiritual, social, economic, and political structures, transforming for the better the human condition for all time to come. These structures freed humans from biases based on differences in gender, race, caste, creed, or national origin, and recognized righteousness and responsibility for one's actions as the only standards to determine an individual's superiority or inferiority. Islam emphasized the role of the family in building individual character from infancy, even during the prenatal stage.

Good and decent laws produce great societal structures, which in turn generate noble individuals, who in turn prefer and promote decency and righteousness as the hallmark of their collective culture. Rose W. Lane, discussing the impact of Muslim life on Europeans, writes:

> But the returning Crusaders brought back to Europe the first idea of a gentleman that Europeans had ever had. Until they invaded the Saracen [a derogative for Syrian, and by extension Arab and Muslim] civilization, they had never known that a strong man need not be brutal. The Saracens were splendid fighters when they fought, but they were not cruel; they did not torture their prisoners, they did not kill the wounded. In their own country, they did not persecute the Christians. They were brave men, but they were gentle. They were honorable; they told the truth, they kept their word.[2]

These Islamic characteristic traits first impressed educated Italians, who were the earliest Europeans to come into contact with Near-Eastern Muslims. The British cherished these Muslim imprints on themselves. Lane adds:

> It is still producing perhaps the finest class of human beings on earth today, the men and women of the British ruling class. It is an ideal that permeates all of American life ... From such dim indications an American can get some idea of the people with whom the Italians were dealing, before and while they were "awakening" Europe ...
>
> All Italians were prospering from trade with the Saracens. Italian merchants, traders, sea-captains, sailors, were constantly meeting men of greater knowledge and wider experiences than theirs, richer men, better dressed, better fed, cleaner and better groomed; men who thought and acted quickly, acted independently. They had better methods of navigating ships, quicker ways of computing costs and adding bills. With incredible swiftness, they dispatched their business affairs over great distances.

No activity of theirs, spiritual, social, economic, or political, was devoid of morality. They had a clear code of conduct in earning their livelihood and in spending it.

Women were free and equipped with a high level of literacy to adopt any decent occupation. In the case of economic need, they were able to move around the world while keeping their high moral character. Members of all non-Muslim minorities, who were often exempt from military service, were protected by the Muslim majority. It was incumbent upon the latter to defend their lives, lands, and liberties. Education at all levels was accessible to all regardless of gender, race, creed or socio-economic status. Slaves too had an ample opportunity to rise even to the level of kingship. The long reign of the Turkish slave dynasty of kings from the eighth to the fourteenth century in Muslim India, and those of the Mamlūk, the Muslim slave kings of Egypt, from the thirteenth to the sixteenth century are a testimony to the pluralism of Islamic societies, which long pre-dated such freedoms anywhere in the West. The renowned historian of Princeton University, Philip Hitti,[3] writes about the Mamlūks: "The bondsmen of yesterday became the army commanders of today and the sultans of tomorrow."

Islam has a very broad concept of worship, which includes any worthy act in any domain of life so long as it is done in accordance with the Divine Guidance, bridging the gap between the moral and the merely legal. In an Islamic polity there is no separation between the moral and the mundane. It thus has brought humanity to its most moderate and balanced state. Islam highlights the role of one's conscience in all one's activities. By removing worship based on a fear of objects of nature such as snakes or monkeys, or indebtedness to creatures like other humans, cows, or other animals, Muslims, in Islam, were able to inculcate in their children a feeling of chivalry and freedom from fear.[4] These values attracted people of diverse races, religions, and ethnic backgrounds into the fold of Islam to form a rare and real rainbow of peoples. All are equal in the sight of God, the only Islamic criterion to judge one's worth is one's righteous behavior in all human affairs. Thus, Muslims were able to establish a societal order completely free from class considerations and immune to any psychological complexes arising from power consciousness or alienation based on learnt helplessness.

Without succumbing to their animal instincts, Muslims were able to internalize and implement their God-given human potential and mission. In their heyday, Muslims made continual progress and unprecedented accomplishments in almost all human activities.

The Islamic culture effectively intervened between extreme forces

engaged in mutual destruction, and thus saved humanity from these trials
and tribulations for centuries. The global feeling of freedom and dignity
on the part of all and sundry brought about a prolonged period of progress and a comprehensive development, which balanced the inner and
outer forces of life. Islam inspired humanity to evolve a middle path between awareness of its self-worth and God-consciousness. It brought
about an order, which gave supremacy to principles of justice over merely
personal preferences, pleasures, and unprincipled passions to possess
property at all costs. It created a balance between extremes of individualism and total self-negation, between the value of human reason and
Divine Revelation, between stark atheistic self-reliance and diseased
dependence on only providential provision without working hard enough
within one's means. It also placed fulfillment of one's own duties and responsibilities before the claiming of one's rights from others. It sought to
remove the confusion between means and ends, without justifying the use
of unfair means to gain so-called "good" ends. Islam refuses to accept
freedom, wealth, power, and control as ultimate ends in themselves but
rather views them merely as a means to some worthy end. By doing so, it
raises the questions of what end and how these necessary means are to be
utilized, bearing in mind that the worthiest goal of a Muslim is to be just
and fair in all spiritual, economic, social, and political dealings with
others, whether Muslim or non-Muslim.

The Islamic values enabled believers to be absolutely clear about
preferred gender roles to protect the family as an essential and fundamental institution, in which spouses did not confront each other with
hostility, but cooperated with each other like the wheels of a smooth
running vehicle. They enabled human intellect and sincere passion to
channel them harmoniously in a constructive rather than destructive
direction. Modesty in appearance, eating, clothing, speaking, and walk-
ing is the responsibility of both sexes so as not to give rise to any laxity
whilst in a pre-marital state or infidelity within marriage.

It is unfortunate that Muslims have not only failed to acquaint their
fellow human beings of their universal faith and illustrious contributions
to world civilization but are also by and large ignorant of their own
golden history. They need to end their isolationism and ghettoization and
interact with people of other faith communities to learn about their value
systems and share with them their own Islamic values in a collective

attempt to address the problems facing humanity, and to be proactive in preventing potential conflicts.

These occasions can serve as effective harbingers of a much-needed atmosphere, that of true interfaith and cross-cultural diversity leading to peace with justice across the globe. They can also significantly contribute to democratic discourses among various civilizations instead of beating the drums of conflict and clashes among them.

As Louay Safi[5] has rightly emphasized in his chapter in this volume, it was the inclusive nature of Islam which led to subsequent exchanges among scholars of all faiths and their willingness to learn from one another in the selfless pursuit of truth.[5] It was the historic interfaith understanding, tolerance, and mutual respect characteristic of Muslim communities that helped them coordinate contemporary knowledge from China, India, the Middle East, North Africa, and Greece. They inherited, critiqued, and further advanced this ancient learning. The Muslim contributions to human civilization led to the European Renaissance of the Elizabethan period, and ultimately inspired the democratic ideals of our constitution as well as the current cross-cultural climate of America.

The sudden end of the Cold War has catapulted the United States into the position of global leadership. Our nation has a choice between becoming a force of freedom and democracy or one yielding to the temptation of the Darwinian "survival of the fittest" with a view to dominating the weaker world. It has a choice between working for the benefit of all or working for the profit of a few, between genuine global cooperation or brute competition, and between peace with justice or peace with force. The prevailing reading of human history leaves us with the impression that everything worthwhile had its origins in Greek or Roman thought, and that the next phase of progress occurred in the sixteenth-century Renaissance. This assumption fails to acknowledge the contributions of other non-Western cultures to world civilization in general and to the reawakening of Europe in particular. Such myopia has often given the religious and commercial media a free hand to stereotype certain communities: Jews, African-Americans, Catholics, Japanese, Communists, and now Muslims and Islam.

One would expect academia to do better in promoting the truth. However, secular academia itself has developed an aversion to discussing the contributions of religious principles of any culture or community.

This attitude denies the latter a fair chance to clear the air of any negative stereotyping generated against them, let alone correct the distortions of history and of human civilization as a whole. The tragic events of September 11, 2001 have made us realize the danger of terrorism and have engendered a sense of vulnerability. At the same time, the American leadership has acted wisely by not isolating itself from the rest of the world, but has begun to engage its people in global affairs. One might disagree with its unilateralism and pre-emptive military actions against weaker nations, yet it has tremendous potential to contribute to peace with justice, which it can do only by attempting to understand the democratic aspirations for basic freedoms, human rights, fairness, and justice for all. Working with Muslim Americans as well as other representative leadership around the Muslim world, the United States can fulfill the goal of establishing a genuinely just and judicious societal order across the globe. Instead of harping on about civilizational clashes, we can engage ourselves in mutual learning from the rich legacy of Islamic culture and the unprecedented technological and administrative contributions the West has made to the modern world.

DILNAWAZ A. SIDDIQUI

NOTES

NOTES TO THE PREFACE

1   H.J. Morowitz, "History's Black
    Hole, *Hospital Practice* (May
    1992), pp.25–31.

2   Robert Briffault, *The Making of
    Humanity* (1938); reproduced in
    *Islamic Science in the Medieval
    Muslim World* (Pakistan:
    Khawarizmi Science Society
    website, November 2001).

NOTES TO THE PROLOGUE

1   H.J. Morowitz, "History's Black
    Hole," *Hospital Practice* (May
    1992), pp.25–31.

2   George Sarton, *Introduction to
    the History of Science*, vol.2
    (Baltimore, MD: Carnegie
    Institute of Washington, William
    & Wilkins, 1947).

3   Robert Briffault, *The Making of
    Humanity* (1938); reproduced in
    *Islamic Science in the Medieval
    Muslim World* (Pakistan:
    Khawarizmi Science Society
    website, November 2001).

NOTES TO CHAPTER ONE

1   http://www.kisarazu.ed.jp/
    alt/handbook/cross_culture.htm
    (Google, 2004).

2   Jerald F. Abraham Dirks, *The

Friend of God (Beltsville, MD:
    Amana Publications, 2002), p.1.

3   http://www.ummah.com/
    forum/archive/index.php/t-
    4689.html, 2004.

4   Al-Fārūqī, Ismāʿīl R, *al-Tawhid:
    Its Implications for Thought and
    Life* (Herndon, VA: The Interna-
    tional Institute of Islamic
    Thought, 1992), pp.78–79.

5   Norman F. Cantor, *The Encyclo-
    pedia of the Middle Ages* (New
    York: Viking, 1999), pp.349–350.

6   SWT: *Subḥānahu wa Taʿalā*: May
    He be praised and may His Trans-
    cendence be affirmed. Said on all
    occasions.

7   Ataullah Siddiqui (ed.), *Ismail Raji
    al-Faruqi, Islam and Other Faiths*
    (Leicester, UK: Islamic Founda-
    tion, 1998), pp.28, 146, 153.

8   Walter Benjamin Franklin Isaac-
    son, *An American Life* (New
    York: Simon & Schuster, 2003),
    p.84.

9   Qur'an, 4:58; 7:29.

NOTES TO CHAPTER TWO

1   René Descartes, *Meditations on
    First Philosophy*, trans. John
    Cottingham (Cambridge, UK:
    Cambridge University Press,
    1986), p.49.

2 Jean-Jacques Rousseau, *The Social Contract*, trans. Maurice Cranston (London: Penguin Books, 1968), p.186.

3 Immanuel Kant, *Critique of Pure Reason*, trans. Norman Kemp Smith (New York: Macmillan, 1929), p.640.

4 Friedrich Nietzsche, *Beyond Good and Evil* (New York: Vintage Books, 1966) p.66.

5 Karl Marx, *The Marx–Engels Reader*, ed. Robert C. Tucker (2nd edn., New York: W.W. Norton, 1978), p.28.

6 Nietzsche, *Beyond Good and Evil*, pp.74–75.

7 Ibid., p. 45.

8 Abu al-Ala al-Mawdudi, *Naẓariyat al-Islam wa Hadyihi* (Jeddah, Saudi Arabia: Dār al-Saʿūdiah, 1985), p.47.

9 Ibid., pp.22–23.

10 Ibid., p.24.

11 Rashid al-Ghanoushi, *al-Ḥuriyāt al-ʿAmmah fī al-Dawlah al-Islāmiyyah* [General Liberties in the Islamic State] (Beirut: Markaz Dirāsāt al-Waḥdah al-Arabiyyah, 1993), p.258.

12 ṢAAS: *Ṣalla Allahu ʿalayhi wa Sallam:* May the peace and blessings of Allah be upon him. This prayer is said by Muslims whenever the name of the Prophet Muhammad is mentioned or whenever he is referred to as the Prophet of Allah.

13 For the full text of the Covenant of Madinah, see Ibn Hishām, *al-Sīrah al-Nabawiyyah* [The Biography of the Prophet] (Damascus: Dār al-Kunūz al-Adabiyyah, n.d.), vol. 1, pp.501–502.

14 Ibid., p. 501.

15 Ibid.

16 Qur'an: 9:97 & 49:14.

17 Ibn Hishām, *al-Sīrah*, p.501.

18 Ibid.

19 Ibid.

20 Muhammad Bin Ahmed, al-Sarakhsi, *Sharḥ Kitāb al-Siyar al-Kabir* (Pakistan: Nusrullah Mansour, 1405 AH), 4:1530.

21 Ibid.

22 Ali ibn Muḥammad al-Māwardī, *al-Aḥkām al-Sulṭāniyyah* (Cairo: Dār al-Fikr, 1983/1401), p.59.

23 Ibid.

24 Ibid.

25 See, Ibn al-Qayyim, *Sharḥ al-Shurūt al-ʿUmariyyah* (Beirut: Dār al-ʿIlm li al-Malāyin, 1961/1381).

NOTES TO CHAPTER THREE

1 The author has offered a perceptive analysis of Māwardī's comprehensive political treatise, explaining how different scholars, before and after Māwardī, dealt with the relationship between reason and Revelation; and how politics, including justice, is connected with revelation, and comparing Islamic and Western thought. He concludes that in the nineteenth and the twentieth centuries, Muslims, after the impact of the Western political

thought, realized the need for a more intellectual orientation of the Islamic political system.

2   Mikhael Hanna, *Politics and Revelation: Mawardi and After* (Edinburgh, Scotland, UK: Edinburgh University Press, 1995).

3   The Prophet sent 30 letters to the Heads of States and tribes, sent 80 delegations, signed 33 treaties, and organized 85 battles and expeditions in defense.

4   Muhammad S. Qureshi, *Foreign Policy of Hadrat Muhammad* (New Delhi: Kitab Bhavan, 1993).

5   Muhammad S. El-Awa, *On the Political System of the Islamic State,* trans. Ahmed Naji al-Imam (Indianapolis, IN: American Trust Publications, 1980).

6   Al-Bukhārī, # 2462, http://www.dorar.net/mhadith.asp.

7   In a brilliant introduction, Mumtaz Ahmad has underlined the need for enunciating an Islamic political theory. Several renowned scholars like Fathi Osman, Khalid Ishaq, Javed Iqbal, Fazlur Rahman, Abdulaziz Sachedina, Ahmad Moussavi, and Jamilah Jimmod have made notable contributions to aspects of Islamic political thought such as the *Bayᶜah* of the Imam, the principle of *Shūrā, Vilayat-i-Faqih, Marja'iyyat-i-taqlid,* the Islamic social order, and jihad.

8   Mumtaz Ahmed (ed.), *State Politics and Islam* (Indianapolis, IN: American Trust Publications,

1986).

9   In this thought-provoking book, the author gives the genesis of an Islamic political system, its objectives and principles, suggesting that ijtihad should continue in it in modern times.

10   El-Awa, *On the Political System of the Islamic State.*

11   The Islamic political system greatly stresses systematic and organizational soundness, hence the need for righteous and effective leadership geared to maintaining peace with justice. Thus, the Ummah is not to be left leaderless under any circumstances.

12   Hamid Enayat, *Modern Islamic Political Thought* (Austin, TX: University of Texas Press, 1982).

13   Attermethe, # 1849, Muslim # 1854 http://www.dorar.net/mhadith.asp.

14   Strictly from the perspective of the Qur'an and Sunnah, the paramount criteria of the head of an Islamic state are piety, an acute sense of accountability to Allah, and the practical implementation of the human rights (*ḥuqūq al-ᶜIbād*).

15   Majid Ali Khan, *The Pious Caliphs* (Safat, Kuwait: Islamic Book Publishers, 1995).

16   That "Scholars like Rashid Riḍa and Mawdudi, who were courageous enough to criticize the policy of ᶜUthmān for retaining Muᶜāwiyah for nearly 20 years as Governor" deserves comment. Those so-

called scholars are not courageous but rather ignorant to criticize ʿUthmān for not dismissing Muʿāwiyah. Muʿāwiyah was described by the Prophet as a knowledgeable Companion and the Prophet prayed for his increased knowledge. Second, he was a very skillful governor, who was given the post at the time of Abū Bakr, and then continued in it during ʿUmar's Caliphate, and neither Caliph dismissed Muʿawiyah. Why should ʿUthmān be criticized for that? We believe nowadays a lot of rumors and you can see how the media fabricate the news and we have a difficult time in correcting it. So how can any human pass judgment on what took place 1400 years ago? Anyone who does is, to say the least, irresponsible.

17 Important aspects covered include: divergence and convergence in Shiʿite and Sunni political concepts, Rashid Riḍa's view of the Islamic state, nationalism, democracy, and socialism, and concepts of *taqiyyah*, martyrdom, and modern constitutionalism

18 Al-Bukhārī, # 6722, http://www.dorar.net/mhadith.asp, the Prophet discouraged requests for nomination.

19 Muhsin Mahdi, *Political Philosophy in Islam* (1991).

20 Abdullah al-Ahsan, *Ummah or Nation?: Identity Crisis in Contemporary Muslim Society* (Leicester, UK: Islamic Foundation, 1992).

21 Al-Būkhārī, # 4844; Muslim # 1783, 1785, 1807, Abū Dawūd # 2349: http://www.dorar.net/mhadith.asp. Although he has dealt with important topics like the concept of the Ummah, the rise of the Muslim nation states, the identity crisis of the Muslims, and the establishment of the Organization of Islamic Conference as an entity for cooperation in political, economic, and social fields, the author has omitted to mention that according to the Madinan Constitution, minorities acceding to it became part of the Ummah and were allowed a share of the booty.

22 Al-Būkhārī # 4609, al-Albānī # 3340 http://www.dorar.net/mhadith.asp.

23 ʿAbdullah ibn Saba' was a Jew who pretended to be a Muslim and attempted to cause problems in the Muslim state. According to some he was not a Muslim.

24 Muslim # 1763 http://www.dorar.net/mhadith.asp.

25 This hadith is weak and not authentic about the suggestion of al-Ḥabbab ibn al-Munthir.

26 Yushau Sodiq, "Imam Malik's Concept of Maslahah: The Consideration of the Common Good," unpublished PhD dissertation (Temple University, Philadelphia, 1992).

27 Ahmed, *State Politics and Islam.*

28 Proctor J. Harris (ed.), *Islam and International Relations* (Durham, NC: Duke University, 1968).

29 Al-Bukhārī, # 6806. http://www.dorar.net/mhadith.asp.

30 Muslim, # 2578. http://www.dorar.net/mhadith.asp.

31 Ibn Taymiyyah, 220/1. http://www.dorar.net/mhadith.asp.

32 Ibn Mājah, # 2494, Attermethe # 2464 http://www.dorar.net/mhadith.asp.

33 Al-Bukhārī # 2558 http://www.dorar.net/mhadith.asp.

34 Hanna, 1995.

35 Māwardī's book or analysis implying that Sharī'ah as an insufficient yardstick for 'adl (justice) is *Kufr* or disbelief. Clearly, Allah said in *Sūrat al-Mā'idah* in the Qur'an: "Today I have completed your religion and perfected my blessing upon you [ISLAM] and I am satisfied with Islam as your religion" (5:3). Anyone who thinks that Islam as a religion is lacking some concepts, clearly implies that he knows better than Allah or Allah forgot something which he has presumptuously found. This concept contradicts the message of Islam and the verse mentioned above.

36 The concept of Imam Mālik's *Maṣlaḥah* is a well-accepted doctrine, underlining the need of the community for ijtihad to suit changing circumstances. According to Shi'ite tradition, ijtihad never stopped, as is evident from Iran's political history in which 'alims have a constitutional role. (The author can be contacted at: Syedahsani@sbcglobal.net.)

37 Muhammad Hamidullah, *The Emergence of Islam* [Lectures at Bahawalpur University, 1963]. Trans.ed. Ambassador Islamic Research Institute in collaboration with the Dawah Academy, Islamabad, International Islamic University, 1993.

38 Hamidullah, *The Emergence of Islam*, pp.155–157. Dr. Hamidullah is the first scholar to suggest the concept of a state within a state, namely, Muslim administration at Makkah, for no matters relating to Muslims were referred to pagans but to the Prophet. This is relevant to the position of Muslim minorities in the West. Ghannouchi, a Tunisian scholar and founder of al-Nahḍah, now residing in London, is opposed to Muslim minorities striving for a separate state as was done in Nigeria and Pakistan, limiting such minorities to the missionary role of *al-'amr bi al-Ma'rūf wa al-nahī 'an al-Munkar* – enjoining good and forbidding evil, converting people to Islam. They should project a good Muslim character as caring neighbors, honest workers, and responsible participants in the political system, making the West a moral and spiritual power in the world, heralding an era of peace,

freedom, equality, honor, dignity, and justice for all.

The Companions set an example of democracy and freedom never repeated in the history of humankind and will never be repeated, even in the USA. The Companions who migrated from Makkah to Madinah would have been considered foreigners according to our current definition of citizenship. They had lived in Madinah for only 10 years when the Prophet died. The people of Madinah were the majority yet they elected Abū Bakr (a foreigner according to our definitions today) to be their ruler. Then ʿUmar was nominated with the agreement of all the people of Madinah, followed by ʿUthmān and ʿAlī. Where in the history of humankind has an immigrant, after only a few years, become the president of a country to which he has migrated? Only Muslims achieved that because Islam teaches them to choose the best and righteous. Yet both Abū Bakr and ʿUmar were from poor, weak, and little-known tribes. We challenge the whole world to give us a similar example. (The author can be contacted at: Syedahsani@sbcglobal.net.).

NOTES TO CHAPTER FOUR

1 Richard Terdiman, "Translator's Introduction" to Pierre Bourdieu, "The Force of Law: Toward a Sociology of the Juridical Field," trans. Richard Terdiman, *The Hastings Law Journal* (July 1987), 38(5)m pp.805–853.

2 Tzvetan Todorov, *Life in Common: An Essay in General Anthropology,* trans. Katherine Golson & Lucy Golson (Lincoln, NB: University of Nebraska Press, 2001).

3 Ibid.

4 Pierre Bourdieu, "The Force of Law: Toward a Sociology of the Juridical Field," trans. Richard Terdiman, *The Hastings Law Journal* (July 1987), 38(5), pp.805–853.

5 Ibid.

6 Terdiman, "Translator's Introduction" to Pierre Bourdieu, "The Force of Law".

7 Pierre Bourdieu, "The Force of Law".

8 A. John Simmons, *The Lockean Theory of Rights* (Princeton, NJ: Princeton University Press, 1992), p.14.

9 Todorov, *Life in Common*.

10 Ibid.

11 Ibid.

12 Norman F. Cantor, *Imagining the Law: Common Law and the Foundations of the American Legal System* (New York: HarperCollins, 1997). "CREDO."

13 Michel Foucault, *Discipline & Punish: The Birth of the Prison,* trans. Alan Sheridan (New York: Vintage Books, 1995), p.22–24, 293–308.

14 Ibid.

15 Ibid.

16 Ibid.

17 Karen Armstrong, *Islam: A Short History* (New York: The Modern Library, 2000), p.202.

18 Ibid.

19 Abdur Rahman I. Doi, *Shari'ah: The Islamic Law* (London: Ṭā Ha Publishers, 1984).

20 Ibid.

21 Ibid.

22 Muhammad Asad, *This Law of Ours and Other Essays* (Gibraltar: Dār al-Andalus, 1987), pp.34–37.

23 Richard Eldridge, *Leading a Human Life: Wittgenstein, Intentionality, and Romanticism* (Chicago: University of Chicago Press, 1997), p.73 (quoting Schiller).

24 L. Carl Brown, *Religion and State: The Muslim Approach to Politics* (New York: Columbia University Press, 2000).

NOTES TO CHAPTER FIVE

1 Ishratullah Khan, *Ehd-e-Mamun Ki Tibbi wa Falsafiyana Kutub Kay Trajim: Ek Tehqiqi Mutalea* [Translation of Medical and Philosophical Documents in the Abbasid Era: A Research Study] (1994), pp.2 & 251.

2 James Burke, *The Day the Universe Changed* (London: BBC, 1985), a companion book serialized on PBS in the late 1980s.

3 Karima Alvi & Susan Douglass, "Science and Religion: The Inseparable Traditions" (Manuscript, 1995), p.9.

4 Marcia Colish, *Medieval Foundations of the Western Intellectual Tradition 400–1400: The Yale Intellectual History of the West* (New Haven, CT: Yale University Press, 1997), pp.129–159.

5 Philip Hitti, *History of the Arabs* (London: Macmillan Education, 1970), pp.363–428.

6 Mehdi Nakhosteen, *Near-Eastern Origins of Western Higher Education* (Boulder, Co: University of Colorado Press, 1964).

7 Owen Gingerish, "Islamic Astronomy," *Scientific American* 254(10) (April 1986), p.74.

8 A. Waheed Yousif, "Lifelong Learning in the Early Abbasid Period" (unpublished PhD diss., Ontario Institute of Studies in Education, University of Toronto, Canada, 1978).

9 Edward Wilson, *Consilience: Unity of Knowledge* (Cambridge, MA: Harvard University Press, 1998).

10 M. AbdulAziz Salim & M. Salahuddin Hilmi, *Islam fi al-Maghrib wa al-Andalus* [Islam in North-West Africa and Spain], ed. Levi Provençal (trans. 1990).

11 Ibn Nadīm, *al-Fehrist*, Arabic–Urdu trans. Ishaq Bhatti (Lahore, Pakistan: Midway Press, 1990).

12 S. Moinul Haq (ed.), *Ibn Khallikan's Wafiyat al-ᶜAᶜyān wa*

Anbā' Abnā' al-Zamān, trans. M.
de Slane (New Delhi: Kitab
Bhavan, 1996), vols.1–7.

13 Jane Norman, *Focus on Asian
Studies: Asian Religion, New
Series* (New York: Asia Society,
2001), vol.2, no.1.

14 N. Khanikoff (trans.), "al-
Khazini's Mizan al-Hikmah" [The
Balance of Wisdom], *The Journal
of the American Oriental Society*,
6 (New Haven, CT: 1859).
Quoted in M. Raziuddin Siddiqi,
Contribution of Muslims to
Scientific Thought (http://www.
centralmosque.com/biographies/s
cience.htm)

15 Readers may also refer to the pre-
conference document prepared for
the regional conference of the
Association of Muslim Social
Scientists (AMSS) (Dallas, Texas,
June 22–23, 2001), pp.61–86.

NOTES TO CHAPTER SIX

1 'Abdullah Yūsuf 'Alī, *The Holy
Qur'an – Translation and
Commentary* (Brentwood, MD:
Amana Corp., 1989), p.1472,
55:1–4.

2 P. Lande, "Science in al-Andalus,"
in *Science: The Islamic Legacy*
(Washington, DC: Aramco,
1988).

3 S. H. H. Nadvi, *Medical Philosophy in Islam and the Contributions of Muslims in the Advancement of Medical Sciences* (Dur-
ban, South Africa: Academia
Centre for Islamic, Near and

Middle Eastern Studies, 1983).

4 M.A. Khan, *Origin and
Development of Experimental
Science* (Dhaka: BITT, 1997).

5 M.R. Mirza & M.I. Siddiqi (eds.),
Muslim Contribution to Science
(Lahore, Pakistan: Kazi Publica-
tions, 1986).

6 M. Saud, *Islam and Evolution of
Science* (Delhi: Adam Publishers,
1994).

7 T.J. Abercrombie, "When the
Moors Ruled Spain," *National
Geographic* (July 1988),
pp.86–119.

8 C.J.M. Whitty, *The Impact of
Islamic Medicine on Post-
Medieval England* (Hyderabad,
India: Islamic Culture, 1999).

9 H.J. Morowitz, "History's Black
Hole," *Hospital Practice* (1992),
pp.25–31.

10 E.G. Brown, *Arabian Medicine*
(Cambridge, UK: Cambridge
University Press, 1962); S.A.R.
Hamdani, *Notable Muslims*
(Karachi, Pakistan: Ferozsons
Press, 1962); M. Ullman, *Islamic
Medicine* (Karachi, Pakistan:
Edinburgh Press, 1978). E. Sav-
age-Smith, *Islamic Culture and
Medical Arts* (Bethesda, MD:
National Library of Medicine,
1994); G. Sarton, *Introduction
to History of Science*, vol.1,
(Washington, DC: Carnegie
Institute; Baltimore, MD: William
& Wilkins, 1927; reprinted
1950); E.A. Myers, *Arabic
Thought and the Western World
in the Golden Age of Islam* (New

York: Funga Publications, 1964),
pp.7–10, 66–77; P. K. Hitti,
History of the Arabs (London:
Macmillan, 1964).

11 Bernard Lewis, *The Middle East*
(New York: Scribner Publications,
1998).

12 S.H. Nasr, *Islamic Science: An
Illustrated Study* (London: World
of Islamic Festival Publishing,
1976).

13 Abercrombie, "When the Moors
Ruled Spain."

14 J. Esposito, *Islam: The Straight
Path* (Oxford, UK: Oxford
University Press, 1998).

15 Nadvi, *Medical Philosophy in
Islam.*

16 Robert Briffault, *The Making of
Humanity* (1938). See, *Islamic
Science in the Medieval Muslim
World* (Pakistan: Khawarizmi
Science Society website, Novem-
ber 2001).

17 Whitty, *The Impact of Islamic
Medicine.*

18 Briffault, *The Making of
Humanity.*

19 H.N. Wasti, *Muslim
Contributions to Medicine*
(Lahore, Pakistan: 1962).

20 H.N. Wasti, "Hospitals are
Owned by Arab Physicians in the
Middle Ages," in *Muslim
Contributions to Science*, ed.
M.R. Mirza & M.I. Siddiqi
(Pakistan: Kazi Publications,
1986).

21 Whitty, *The Impact of Islamic
Medicine.*

22 Wasti, *Muslim Contributions to*

Medicine; A. Ali, *The Arab–
Muslim Legacy to Ophthalmol-
ogy* (Hyderabad, India: Islamic
Culture, 1999).

23 *Encyclopedia Britannica*, vol.1,
Micropedia (1983), p.37.

24 *Muslim Contributions to
Chemistry* (FSTC, 2003).
www.muslimheritage.com

25 Khan, *Experimental Science.*

26 David Tschnaz, "Jabir Ibn Hyyan
and Arab AlChemists: Makers
of Modern Chemistry",
www.islamonline.net/English/Scie
nce/200108/article

27 A. Zahur, *Muslim History
570–1950* (Gaithersburg, MD:
ZMD Corp., 2000).

28 Lande, "Science in al-Andalus;"
A. Z.Ashoor, "Muslim Medieval
Scholars and their Work," *The
Islamic World Medical Journal*
(1984). H.R. Khan, "Contribut-
ion of Muslims to Medicine and
Science up to the Middle of 13th
Century," *Journal of Islamic
Medical Association*, 14 (1982),
pp.111—114.

29 M. Levey, *Early Arabic Pharmacology* (Leiden, The Netherlands:
E.J. Brill, 1973), pp.68-70.

30 Saud, *Islam and Evolution of
Science.*

31 G. Sarton, G., *Introduction to
History of Science*, vol. 2
(Washington, DC: Carnegie
Institute; Baltimore, MD : William
& Wilkins, 1931;reprinted 1950).

32 A.A. Salam, *Islam and Science*
(Trieste, Italy: Institute of
Theoretical Physics).

33 H. Sayeed, *Muslim Scholars*
    (Pakistan: National Science
    Council, Internet Edition 2000).

34 *Encyclopedia Britannica*, 1983, II.
    Macropedia, vol. 9 (1983),
    pp.198–199.

35 S. A. Ahsani, "Al-Mawardi's
    Political Paradigm: Principles of
    Islamic Political System" (n.d.)

36 *Encyclopedia Britannica*, III.
    Macropedia, vol.9 (1983),
    pp.147—149.

37 Sayeed, *Muslim Scholars*.

38 Salam, *Islam and Science*.

39 Herbert H. Rowen, *A History of
    Early Modern Europe 1500–1815*
    (New York: Holt, Rinehart &
    Winston, 1960).

40 Al-Hassan, Ahmady and Hill,
    Donald, *Islamic Technology – An
    Illustrated History* (Cambridge,
    UK: Cambridge University Press,
    1988).

41 Hitti, *History of the Arabs*.

42 Manzoor S. Alam, "A Critical
    Appreciation of Arab Human
    Development Report,"
    (unpublished work, 2002).

NOTES TO CHAPTER SEVEN

1   Dudley Seers, "The Meaning of
    Development," *International
    Development Review* (1969),
    pp.3–4.

2   UNDP (United Nations
    Development Program), *Human
    Development Report 1991*, (New
    York: Oxford University Press,
    1991).

3   Muhammad Muhsin Khan, *The

    Translation of the Meanings of
    Sahih al-Bukhari* (Beirut: Dārul
    Arabia, 1985), vol.3, Hadith
    Number 286, p.162.

4   Ibn Mājah, *Sunan Ibn Mājah*
    (Riyadh: Sharikah al-Ṭibāʿah al-
    ʿArabiyyah as-Saʿūdiah, 1984),
    vol.2, p.7.

5   Ibn Mājah and Bayhaqī, *al-
    Tirmidhī* (Alim CD, Release 4,
    1996), Hadith Number 218.
    www.islsoftware.com.

6   ʿAlī, ʿAbdullah Yūsuf, *The
    Meaning of the Glorious Qur'an*
    (Cairo: Dārul Kitāb al-Maṣrī,
    1934), vol.1, 2:76, fn.83.

7   Bukhārī, p. 52:112; Cairo; Cited in
    Muhammad Umar Chapra, *Objec-
    tives of the Islamic Economic
    Order*, in Khurshid Ahmad (ed.),
    Islam: Its Meaning and Message
    (London: Islamic Foundation,
    1980).

8   Muhammad Asad, *The Principles
    of State and Government in Islam*
    (Gibralter: Dār al-Andalus, 1980).

9   *U.S. Census, Current Population
    Survey, March 1999 and 2000*
    (U.S. Bureau of Census, 2000).

10 Ibid.

11 Ibid.

12 Urban Institute, *Millions Still Face
    Homelessness in a Booming
    Economy*; http://www.urban.org/
    news/pressrel/pr000201.html
    (2000).

13 Mayors' 16th Annual Survey on
    "Hunger and Homelessness in
    America's Cities" Finds Increased
    Levels of Hunger, Increased

Capacity to Meet Demand (USCM, 2000); http://www.usmayors.org/uscm/news/press_releases/documents/hunger_release.htm

14 CHPNP, *Hunger in the U.S.* (Boston, MA: Tufts University Center on Hunger, Poverty, and Nutrition Policy, 2001); http://hunger.tufts.edu/us.html.

15 USDA, *Prevalence of Food Insecurity and Hunger*, by State, 1996–98 (USA: U.S. Department of Agriculture, 1998).

16 UNDP (United Nations Development Program), *Human Development Report 2000* (New York: Oxford University Press, 2000).

17 BLS (Bureau of Labor Statistics), *Value of the Federal Minimum Wage, 1938–1997* (USA: U.S. Department of Labor, 2000).

18 Edward N. Wolff, *Economics of Poverty, Inequity, and Discrimination* (Cincinnati, OH: Southwestern Publishing, 1997).

19 Chuck Collins, Betsy Leonard-Wright, & Holly Sklar, *Shifting Fortunes: The Perils of the Growing American Wealth Gap* (Boston, MA: United for a Fair Economy, 1999).

20 Donald Barlett & James Steele, *America: Who Really Pays the Taxes?* (New York: Simon & Schuster, 1994).

21 Mark Wilhelm, "Estimates of Wealth Tax" (unpublished paper, Pennsylvania State University, University Park, 1998).

22 Bruce Ackerman & Anne Alstott, *The Stakeholder Society* (New Haven, CT: Yale University Press, 1999).

NOTES TO CHAPTER EIGHT

1 Available statistics reveal that American Muslims have an average per capita income ranging between $35,000 and $45,000, well over the national average of $24,000 to $27,000.

2 The CRA played an important role in the development of community banks, allowing the community banks to mobilize the community savings and reinvent these savings in the community.

3 Islamic banks, for example, should abide by chartering requirements, capital adequacy, deposit insurance, and restrictions on asset holdings. The same set of regulations also applies to non-banking institutions like insurance companies, pension funds, real estate agencies, and mutual funds.

4 Because Islamic banks are more akin to finance companies, it may be useful to adopt the same regulations established by the Securities Exchange Commission (these include type of securities, risk factors, internal control, and performance indicators).

5 Since Islamic banks guarantee demand deposits only, a 100% required reserve on demand deposit would help reduce the problems of asset-liability mismatch caused by unexpected

demand deposit withdrawals.

6   The GLBA made two major
changes. First, it allowed bank
holding companies to merge with
insurance and securities companies and cross-sell their products.
Second, it allowed bank holding
companies that did not merge to
underwrite securities, selling or
underwriting insurance, and make
equity investments in business
firms.

NOTES TO THE EPILOGUE

1   Ibrahim Madkour, "Past, Present,
and Future," in J.R.Hayes, *The
Genius of Arab Civilization:
Source of Renaissance,* 2nd edn.
(Cambridge, MA: MIT Press,
1983), pp.243–246.

2   Rose W. Lane, *Islam and the
Discovery of Freedom* (with an
introduction and commentary by
Imad-ad-Dean Ahmad).

(Bethesda, MD: The Minaret of
Freedom Institute; Beltsville, MD:
Amana Publications, 1997),
pp.47–48.

3   Philip K. Hitti, *History of the
Arabs,* 10th edn. (New York:
Macmillan, 1986), p.672.

4   S. AbulHasan Nadvi, *Insani
Duniya par Musalmanon kay
Urooj-o-Zawal ka Asar* [The
Impact of the Rise and Fall of
Muslims on Human Civilization],
8th edn. (Karachi, Pakistan:
Majlis-e-Nashariaat-e-Islam,
1974).

5   Louay Safi, "Overcoming the
Religious-Secular Divide: Islam's
Contribution to Civilization."
Presented at the 2001 AMSS
Regional Conference, Dallas,
Texas, June 22–23.

INDEX

LIST OF CONTRIBUTORS

AbdulHamid AbuSulayman, PhD
President, International Institute of Islamic Thought
Editor-in-Chief, American Journal of Islamic Social Sciences (AJISS)

M. Basheer Ahmed, MD
Former Professor of Psychiatry, South-Western Medical School,
University of Texas, Dallas

Syed A. Ahsani
Former Ambassador of Pakistan

Abdel-Hameed M. Bashir, PhD
Professor of Economics, University of Louisana, LA

Louay M. Safi, PhD
Executive Director, Leadership Development Center, ISNA
Former President, Association of Muslim Social Scientists (AMSS)

Mohammed Sharif, PhD
Professor of Economics, University of Rhode Island, Kingston, RI

Dilnawaz A. Siddiqui, PhD
Emeritus Professor of Communication, Clarion University of
Pennsylvania

Peter Wright, JD
Attorney at Law, Pittsburgh, PA